CHRISTMAS COMPANION

CHRISTMAS COMPANION

GLORIA NICOL

PHOTOGRAPHS BY
MARIE-LOUISE AVERY

a Salamander book
Published by Salamander Books Limited
LONDON

A SALAMANDER BOOK

Published by Salamander Books Limited
129-137 York Way, London N7 9LG,
United Kingdom

1 3 5 7 9 8 6 4 2

© Salamander Books Ltd. 1994

ISBN 0 86101 733 1

All correspondence concerning the content of
this volume should be addressed to
Salamander Books Ltd.

CREDITS
Managing Editor: Anne McDowall
Copy Editor: Veronica Sperling
Designer: Bill Mason
Photographer: Marie-Louise Avery
Home Economist: Maxine Clark
Stylist: Gloria Nicol
Indexer: Alison Leach
Colour Reproduction:
P & W Graphics PTE Ltd., Singapore
Printed in Italy

ONTENTS

INTRODUCTION

The birth of Jesus is celebrated by millions of people all over the world, with many of the rituals and traditions of the present day being rooted in customs that began thousands of years ago.

Christmas was not celebrated as a festival at all until AD353 and nobody can be absolutely sure as to the precise date of Christ's birth. Pope Julius I set the date that we now recognise as Christmas Day, and 25th December became the official day to celebrate Jesus's birthday. By settling for this date, the Christian festival merged with the already well-established pagan midwinter celebrations, the old customs lingering on and becoming absorbed into the new Christian celebrations.

To the peoples of the ancient world, winter was an especially bleak and threatening time. Many believed that the sun itself had died and might never return. The midwinter celebrations held the promise of spring and rebirth and involved feasting, drinking, dancing, gift-giving, holding of parties and general merriment and revelry. Many of these more lighthearted elements of the pagan festival became incorporated into the Christian festival. Feasting was no longer gleeful gluttony, food was shared with others in the true Christian spirit. Both ancient Roman and Victorian households gave gifts to the poor.

Although Christmas Eve and Christmas Day are the main focus of the festival, the entire Christmas period is surrounded by many tales and traditions. Other days within the Christmas calendar hold particular significance in different countries around the world. In Germany, The Netherlands and Poland, St Nicholas, the patron saint of children, brings gifts for them on 6th December as a reward for good behaviour throughout the year. In Sweden, St Lucia's Day is celebrated on 13th December, when the oldest daughter of the family dresses in a long white robe and wears a garland of evergreens and candles on her head. It is her duty to serve the family with a breakfast of coffee and sweet-scented saffron cakes. The Eve of Epiphany celebrates the imminent arrival of the three wise men at the stable where Jesus was born, bringing with them gifts of gold, frankincense and myrrh. Spain and France mark the event with special cakes and crowns to wear. Christmas is a time to celebrate family life and friendship, hospitality and gift-giving, warmth of heart and home and of greetings and goodwill.

CHRISTMAS DECORATIONS

Each year, as the ornaments and baubles are unearthed from the back of the cupboard, where they were carefully packed away, almost a year before, and we begin to prepare to decorate our homes for the festivities ahead, we are in fact taking part in a ritual that predates Christmas and has evolved from earlier pagan celebrations.

For the festival of Saturnalia, the people of ancient Rome lit candles to symbolize the rebirth of the year and decorated their houses with laurel sprigs and other greenery. Evergreens, because of their ability to keep their leaves even through the dead of winter, were thought to possess special powers of eternal life and were given as gifts and taken into the home to make garlands for decorations. The Druids, who believed that everything in the natural world was divine, placed evergreen decorations in the house to provide a safe haven for tree spirits during the harsh days of midwinter. The spirits, normally unwilling to cooperate with humans, were allegedly prepared to make a truce in return for this protection given to them over the Christmas period, but only on condition that they were released again to their natural habitat as soon as the festivities were over.

Holly and mistletoe were especially prized for their ability to produce their fruits in winter when all else is bare. To the Romans, holly signified good health in the year ahead and the renewal of life. For the Druids, it was mistletoe that held a special place and was thought to protect the home and ensure the fertility of its occupants.

Before the introduction of Christmas trees, a kissing bunch would have taken pride of place as the central decoration in many households in England and America. Made of two bisecting hoops of metal or wood, the kissing bunch was decorated with holly and ivy, ribbons, fruits and nuts, with a spray of mistletoe hanging down below it. For every kiss given under it, one of the white berries was removed from the sprig of mistletoe until all the berries had gone and the kissing had to stop.

The commercialization of Christmas began in earnest in the Victorian Era, making way for the great variety of seasonal merchandise that is available to us today. Whether we make decorations to adorn our houses at this time of year, or buy them ready made, we are in essence still following an age-old tradition, which has always held its own special magic.

CHRISTMAS TREES

The Christmas tree, laden with shining glass baubles, glinting and turning in the light, and with presents wrapped and piled high beneath it waiting to be opened, is always an enchanting sight to behold.

The origin of the Christmas tree can be traced back to the eighth century when Boniface, the English missionary to Germany, introduced a fir tree decorated in homage to the Christ child. Trees had played an important part in religion before this, but the fir now replaced the sacred oak, its triangular shape with three points representing the Holy Trinity, with God the Father at the top, and the Son of God and the Holy Spirit at the two lower points.

The day before Christmas became devoted to the memory of Adam and Eve who were commemorated as saints in the calendars of the Greek Orthodox church and other Eastern churches which spread to the west.

In the Middle Ages plays were performed in the open in public places, such as large squares and in front of churches, to tell the story of creation. In Germany these plays were known as Paradise Plays and the only prop used was a variation on the old symbol for Yule tree, an evergreen fir hung with apples, which represented the Tree of Knowledge in the Garden of Eden. Centuries later the plays were banned by the church for a time and the trees were taken inside the homes at Christmas time and the custom of decorating them became gradually more elaborate, with sweetmeats, fruit and candles.

In 16th century Germany, city merchants would carry a fir tree decorated with paper flowers through the streets on Christmas Eve. A great feast was held in the market square, followed by dancing around the Christmas tree, and finally the tree was ceremonially burned.

During the 17th and 18th centuries Christmas trees were used in other ways. Sometimes only the tips of the branches were used, often hung upside down, especially over doorways. Some people took fir branches and fixed them to wooden pyramids, which were then decorated, usually with paper roses, nuts and apples. Christmas trees were from the start more popular in the countries of northern Europe than in the southern Catholic countries, for whom the nativity crib is still the centrepiece of their Christmas decorations.

In England, German merchants living near Manchester before 1840 are said to have decorated Christmas trees for their children, but it wasn't until Prince Albert, the German husband of Queen Victoria, introduced the custom to England that the practice became fashionable. In the 1948 edition of the Illustrated London News, the Royal Family were portrayed at Windsor gathered around their tree and from then on the Christmas tree became an essential part of the English Christmas, from where the custom soon spread to America.

CHOOSING A TREE

Nothing can beat the look and fragrance of a real Christmas tree. Before going out to buy one, consider the size of the room and how much space the decorated tree is going to take up. Norway Spruce is one of the most popular varieties and is usually the cheapest, but it does tend to shed needles all over the floor. There are other varieties that hold their needles better, such as Nordmann and Noble firs, but they are generally more expensive. The firs and pines keep their needles better than spruce.

If your tree decorations mainly hang down from the branches, look for a variety of tree which is open enough for them to dangle and turn without getting stuck on the branches below. Alternatively, if your decorations need to sit on top of the branches, you could choose a type with a denser shape.

It is essential that cut trees should be fresh when purchased. The needles should not be dull and dried up, the branches should bend easily without snapping off and the trunk should be sticky with sap. The outer needles should not fall off when the tree is gently shaken.

After you have bought your tree cut about 2.5 cm (1 in) of the trunk, if possible, to open up the pores and keep it outside or in a cool garage, standing in a bucket of water for a few days. When you bring the tree indoors, try to keep it in a water-holding stand or wedge it in a bucket with pebbles, small stones or screwed up newspaper (not earth or sand), and place it away from direct heat. Keep the container topped up with water each day so the tree stays green and fresh right through to the twelfth night.

CHRISTMAS LIGHTS

Martin Luther, leader of the Reformation movement in the 16th century, was reputedly the first to put candles on the tree after he looked up at a starry sky from beneath a wood of tall pines and wished to create the magical scene he had witnessed as the stars twinkled through the trees.

These days, electric lights are a safer and less troublesome way to illuminate a Christmas tree and look pretty used en masse in single colours. You will need a length of 20 lights for a tree up to 1.6 m (5 ft) and 40 or more for a tree bigger than this. Always check that the lights are working properly before putting them on the tree. Arrange them evenly around the tree before hanging any of the other decorations in place and fix them with twists of short wires or green sewing thread to keep the flex looking tidy.

LEFT: The decorations, carefully packed away the year before, are taken out of storage ready for the festive season ahead. As the fragrance of a real Christmas tree wafts its way through the house you really know that celebrations have begun.

TREE DECORATIONS

RIGHT: Simple household materials can be made into stunning tree decorations. The peg fairies, made from old-fashioned wooden clothes pegs and fabric scraps and oddments, each have their own individual characters.

The earliest Christmas tree decorations were home made; small glass beads from chandeliers were strung together to garland the tree, and fruits, gingerbreads and paper roses were hung on their branches. It was not until the end of the 19th century that tree decorations became widely available to buy, ready made. Now, each year, the shops are so full of every kind and style of decoration to buy that we are spoilt for choice.

Home-made decorations still have their own special charm and making them is an enjoyable part of the Christmas preparations. The peg fairies and metallic stars, shown here, are made from simple household materials using small scraps and oddments of metallic fabrics, card and ribbon in rich colours to catch the light and sparkle on the Christmas tree.

DOLLY PEG FAIRIES

You will need: old-fashioned wooden clothes pegs, scraps of metallic fabrics, lengths of ribbon, assorted oddments of braids and trimmings, beads and sequins, embroidery threads, felt tip pens, glue.

Draw the features for the face on the top of a peg to make the fairy's head, with just a few simple marks using felt tip pens. Apply a small amount of glue to the top and sides of the head and lay strands of embroidery thread across it to make

the hair, leaving the bottom edge slightly ragged and uneven.

Cut 2 semicircles of fabric for the frock, approximately 12 cm (5 in) across and the depth of the peg deep, with a gently curved hem line. Cut out a small semicircle at the top to make a neck opening and glue the fabric pieces together down the sides, leaving the neck opening, and leave to dry. Apply a small amount of glue to the 'bodice' part of the peg before pushing it through the neck opening of the dress, pressing the fabric to the glue and gathering in any fullness in the fabric. Wrap a length of ribbon around the bodice and tie in a bow at the back, to hold it all together. Glue a small length of metallic braid around the head to make a garland. Paint the tips of the peg ends to make slippers then complete the fairy using beads stuck with glue around her hemline and sewn around the bodice ribbon, as required.

METALLIC BALL GARLAND

You will need: 2.5 cm (1 in) cotton wool moulds or polystyrene balls, cord to the required length, gold and bronze spray paint, a bradawl.

Spray the cotton mould balls in batches of the 2 colours and leave them to dry. Push the bradawl through the middle of each ball then thread them onto the cord, alternating the colours and spacing them evenly approximately 8 cm (3¼ in) apart.

METALLIC STARS

You will need: copper mesh pan scourers, metallic card, lengths of ribbon and cord, a selection of pretty beads.

Cut out 2 star shapes in card to fit within the scourer circle (if you are making several decorations it is worth making a template to draw around first). Make 2 holes spaced 1 cm (½ in) apart in the middle of each card star. With the right side of one of the card stars facing you, thread the ends of a length of ribbon 36 cm (14 in) long through each of the holes to the wrong side.

Thread these ends through the pan scourer, pushing them through the mesh, then thread them through another card star to make the front of the decoration. Tie the ends of the ribbon into a bow. Thread beads onto a long length of cord and pull the cord through the middle of the mesh of the scourer from the bottom to the top. Tie the ends with a knot at the top to make a hanging loop.

ABOVE LEFT: The dolly peg fairies can be decorated with different beads, ribbon and braid oddments to make each one unique. LEFT: The materials you will need to make the metallic star, which include a metallic pan scourer. ABOVE: The star decoration ready to be hung on the Christmas tree.

RIGHT: These decorative stars are made from copper wire, bent into shape and then bound with sisal string until completely covered.
FAR RIGHT: After the stars are sprayed with paint, raffia tassels are made to hang below them. Here, the colours of the stars and the tassels have been reversed.

BELOW RIGHT: For the ticking baubles fabric strips are cut on the bias to stop the edges from fraying.
FAR RIGHT: When the baubles are entirely covered with the ticking fabric a hanging loop and a ribbon bow is attatched to each one.

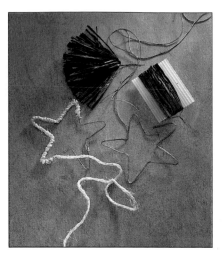

then wind it all round the ball in a random fashion until the ball is completely covered, finishing off and joining on new strips of fabric with glue. Take a 50 cm (19½ in) length of ribbon, fold it in half, then tie a loop 9 cm (3½ in) from the folded end. Tie the ends of the ribbon into a bow and attach this to the top of the bauble to make the hanging loop, using glue and a glass-headed pin pushed through the middle of the bow into the ball.

RAFFIA STARS

You will need: copper wire, sisal string, glue, raffia, spray paint, gold cord, pendant fittings for the tops of the tassels (optional).

Bend a length of copper wire into a star shape, approximately 11 cm (4¼ in) across with 5 points, cutting the ends to overlap by 1 cm (½ in) where they meet and gluing them together. Fix the end of a length of string to the star with a blob of glue, then wind it tightly over and along the wire until the string completely covers it, fastening off the end with more glue. Spray both sides of the star with spray paint and leave it to dry.

Make a tassel by winding raffia around a piece of card 8 cm (3¼ in) long. Thread a length of raffia through all the thicknesses at one end of the card, tie it tightly and remove the card. Bind several times around the tassel 1.5 cm (¾ in) from the top, using a length of raffia, tie the ends together and trim them short. Cut and straighten the end of the tassel then finish it off at the top with a pendant fitting, if

required. Join the tassel to the bottom of the star using sewing thread and a needle. Finish off the decoration with a hanging loop at the top made from gold cord.

TICKING BAUBLES

You will need: ticking fabric, 7 cm (2¾ in) cotton wool moulds or polystyrene balls, glue, lengths of ribbon, a bradawl, glass-headed pins.

Cut the ticking into bias strips 1.2 cm (½ in) wide. Join the end of a strip to a ball with a blob of glue

TICKING BOWS

You will need: ticking fabric, fine reel wire, sewing thread.

Cut bias strips in ticking 4 cm (1½ in) wide and 80 cm (31½ in) long. Place a length of fine wire down the long edge of a fabric strip on the wrong side and turn 5 mm (¼ in) of fabric over to cover it. Machine stitch the turning down with a zig-zag stitch. Wire the other edge in the same way. Trim the ends into points and hem them without wire.

LEFT: Baubles and bows in red and green ticking stripes and tasselled raffia stars bring a fresh look to the traditional Christmas tree. The baubles are made from lightweight cotton or polystyrene balls, which are covered with strips of fabric. They will not be too heavy for even the finest branches of the tree.

Wreaths

A Christmas wreath hung at the doorway offers a seasonal welcome to friends and visitors. The custom can be traced back to ancient Rome when, as part of their New Year celebrations, branches of evergreens were exchanged as gifts by the Romans to symbolize good health. To make the branches more decorative they were bent round into rings and displayed at the entrance of the home in order to increase the chances of a healthy household in the coming year. Nowadays, we tend to provide a wreath for our own home, but if we chose to follow the custom in its original form we would only hang a wreath that had been given to us as a gift.

A star wreath makes an unusual alternative to the traditional ring. The shape is made with a frame using wire coathangers covered with a layer of damp sphagnum

moss to help keep the flowers and foliage fresh for the duration of the festivities. For our star wreath we used just one kind of foliage, Laurustinus (*Viburnum tinus*), and added Christmas roses and lichen-covered larch twigs. To finish off the wreath, it is worth splashing out on a really special piece of ribbon, which can make even a simple wreath look spectacular.

STAR WREATH

You will need: 3 wire coat hangers, sphagnum moss, foliage, flowers, garden twine, a reel of mossing wire, stub wires, glue, a length of ribbon.

To make the wire frame, cut the 2 pointed ends off each of the coat hangers using wire cutters. Bend the pointed ends into sharper points if they are rounded and measure down each side from the point, cutting them all to the same length. Take 5 of these wire Vs and lay them down flat to take the shape of a star, then bend the ends back approximately 2.5 cm (1 in), at an angle, so that each end overlaps with the next one to form the star's inside corners. Glue the overlaps together and bind them with reel wire to hold them firm.

Leave the sphagnum moss to soak in a bucket of water for a while then squeeze out the excess water. Open out the moss and bind it in handfuls to the frame, using

garden twine. This covering of moss needs to be kept fairly light-weight to prevent the weight of the finished wreath pulling the frame out of shape.

Cut the foliage into short lengths and bind several stems together with fine reel wire to make small bunches. Arrange them close together around the mossed frame, pointing and overlapping them in one direction and pushing the stems into the moss to attach them, until it is completely covered. Use lengths of stub wire to hold them in place more firmly if necessary. Cut the flower stems short and arrange them amongst the foliage. Push the stems into the moss and fix them in place using

LEFT: The Christmas wreath is a quintessential symbol of the season and a star-shaped one makes an unusual alternative to the traditional circle. We decorated our wreath with white Christmas roses and lichen-covered twigs but other materials could be used instead. Tiny kumquats and tartan bows would make a delicate and colourful choice or, as a practical alternative, cover the mossed base with small bunches of fresh herbs, such as thyme, purple sage and rosemary for an aromatic wreath to hang in the kitchen.

U-shaped pieces of stub wire pushed over the stems, through the moss to the back of the wreath and then fastened off. The larch twigs on the wreath shown in the picture were attached in the same way, by pushing them in between the foliage into the moss, and were held in place more securely with pieces of stub wire.

To hang the wreath, make a loop out of stub wire and attach it to the back of the top point. Finish the wreath with a ribbon bow, again attached with wire.

 GARLANDS

RIGHT: A decorated fireplace looks resplendent garlanded with greenery, fruits and taffeta ribbon. Spray foliage with water at regular intervals to keep it looking fresh. FAR RIGHT: The foliage is bound with reel wire to a core of garden twine to form a leafy rope that can be made to any length.

Garlands are easy to make and look stunning twining around the bannister rail of a staircase, hung over a doorway or swagged across a fireplace. One simple technique can be used to make a garland of any length using fresh foliage embellished with nuts and seasonal fruits. When choosing your foliage, go for a combination of different shaped, sized and textured leaves such as blue pine, bay and skimmia. For the garland shown in the picture the basic rope of leaves was made from groups of berried ivy, Laurustinus and Portugese laurel, which was then decorated with limes, small pomegranates and lychees to create a rich, burnished effect. Bows of shot taffeta finished it off at each end and covered the fixing points.

FIREPLACE GARLAND
You will need: several different kinds of foliage, a variety of fruits, nuts and seedheads to decorate, garden twine, a reel of mossing wire, stub wires, glue, a length of ribbon.

Measure the length for the finished garland with a double thickness of garden twine, allowing extra for it to drape slightly between the fixing points. Cut the different kinds of foliage into lengths, approximately 14 cm (5½ in) long, cutting the bushy varieties so they make small bunches and joining three or four lengths of any finer single-stemmed types together with reel wire to make them more substantial.

Beginning at one end, bind the foliage to the twine using reel wire, pointing all the stems towards the

LEFT: As well as limes, lychees and pomegranates, other seasonal fruits such as apples and small oranges, nuts and cones can be added to the garland. Use the same method as described for wiring other kinds of fruits. For brazils and walnuts push the end of a stub wire into the eye of the nut and apply a blob of glue to hold it in place; for hazelnuts, pecans and almonds, bend the end of the wire into a circle and glue to the base of the nut.

beginning and laying each new piece overlapping the last. Arrange the different types of foliage in blocks approximately 10 cm (4 in) deep and in sequence all along the twine, to the other end.

Next prepare the fruits for fixing to the garland. To wire the pomegranates, push a length of stub wire through the base, about a quarter way up the fruit, bend the ends to meet each other and twist them together, leaving one long end. Push another wire through the fruit at right angles to the first and twist the ends together. Finally wind the two long ends together.

Wire the fruits so that they face in different directions and will be displayed at different angles to add variety and show off their best sides. The limes and lychees can be wired in the same way, taking extra care with the lychees to bend the wires gently, to prevent the soft flesh from tearing.

Lay the garland down flat and arrange the fruits amongst the leaves, dotted along in groups of three, then push the wires through the garland to the back and wind the ends around it to hold them in place. Make loops out of stub wire and attach them to the back of the garland at each end. Tie two bows in ribbon and fix in place with lengths of stub wire threaded through the back of each one.

ADVENT CALENDAR

The four weeks of Advent that precede Christmas are a time of activity and preparation, in anticipation of the greatest of Christian festivals. Marking each day of the countdown is a wonderful way for the family to share the

RIGHT: An advent calendar adds to the excitement of the impending celebrations. To mark each day from the 1st of December to Christmas Eve, there is a tiny parcel to open containing a chocolate or small gift.

excitement together. In German-speaking countries Advent wreaths are common and are decorated with four candles, one to represent each of the four Sundays before Christmas Day. On the first Sunday, the first candle is lit, on the second, two are lit, and so on, until all four candles are ceremoniously lit and allowed to burn down together on the last Sunday. Sometimes children are given Advent candles, which are marked with 24 divisions, one to be burned on each day until Christmas Eve.

Our framed Advent calendar is made up of 24 tiny parcels, each individually and exquisitely wrapped with a sweet or small gift inside. Ordinary boxes, found around the house, can be put to good use if they are wrapped and decorated, but you can also make some of the more unusual shaped boxes yourself, to add to the variety.

You will need: 24 small boxes in various shapes, 24 sweets or small gifts, a frame approximately 33 cm x 40.5 cm (13 in by 16 in) (without glass), gold and copper spray paint, metallic card, scraps of ribbon and wrapping paper, gold felt tip pen, tissue paper, glue, Velcro, star beads or card stars.

Collect the boxes together and decorate them in different ways; spray some of them with gold and copper paint, stick pieces of foil onto the sides and use a gold felt tip pen to draw simple stripe and border patterns around them. Wrap up those boxes which aren't in good enough condition but try to use boxes which after opening will still be intact so they can be left on the calendar and still look decorative. Glue a piece of tissue paper to the inside base of each box and place the gift inside, then close and finish each parcel with decorative ribbon tied in a bow.

Spray the frame gold. Cut a piece of metallic card to fit the

frame and arrange the parcels on it. Stick them in place using small pieces of Velcro stuck with glue to both surfaces, so the parcels can be removed for opening and then be put back on when the gift has been removed. Any wrapped parcels which after opening don't look good enough to be left on the calendar can be replaced by a star bead or card star with a piece of Velcro glued to the back of it. Frame the card with parcels attached to complete the calendar. Open one parcel each day up to

Christmas Day and remove the treats inside, then replace the parcel without the ribbon, leaving the lids open and the crumpled tissue paper showing within.

The fancy-shaped boxes are easy to make. Draw them onto thin card copying the templates shown on pages 92-93.

LONG HEXAGONAL BOX
Score all the fold lines on the right side of the card with a pointed implement and fold along the score lines. Decorate the box at this stage, if required. Bring the long ends together and glue the tab under the other edge where they meet, to form a faceted tube. Push in the tabs and close the lids at top and bottom.

PYRAMID BOX
Make the box in the same way as the long hexagonal box up to completion of the decoration. Bring the sides of the triangles together to form the pyramid and push the tab through the slit, to hold it in place. Fold in the flaps and close the base of the box.

SHORT HEXAGONAL BOX
Make in the same way as the long hexagonal box.

FAR LEFT: The hexagonal and pyramid-shaped boxes are easy to make from scratch and add variety when used with other small containers found around the home. LEFT: Every tiny parcel contains a treat for the person who opens it. The boxes can be left on the calendar when the goodies have been removed.

CHRISTMAS CRACKERS

For many of us, pulling Christmas crackers during the main festive meal is an essential part of the celebrations and the traditional way to decorate the Christmas table. Tom Smith, an Englishman, is credited with the

RIGHT: Home-made crackers can be filled with unusual and useful items that you won't find in bought varieties, like the small tea infuser shown here. A few star sequins were put inside as well to make the bang even more dramatic.

invention of the cracker in the early 1840s after he visited Paris, where he saw, for the first time, bon-bons wrapped in brightly coloured papers with the ends twisted together. This impressed him so much that on his return he began to develop the idea, incorporating it with the Chinese tradition of placing mottoes in with fortune cookies.

The first crackers were simply a slip of paper bearing a motto curled around a piece of candy, wrapped with coloured, transparent paper. They proved to be a great success. One night, as Tom Smith was sitting in front of a log fire, a piece of wood burning in the hearth let off a loud crack which startled him and he realized that this was the extra element he needed, so he created the cracker snap to make them go off with a bang and add to the party spirit. Eventually the sweets were replaced by lucky charms and tiny gifts, mottoes by jokes and riddles, and tightly folded paper hats were introduced.

Making home-made crackers yourself means that the gifts to fill them can be chosen to suit individual family members or friends, adding a special personal touch.

You will need: a piece of thin card 20 cm x 36 cm (8 in x 14¼ in) for each cracker, a craft knife, cracker snaps, small gifts, an assortment of ribbons, braids, beads etc. to decorate, glue.

Cut out a shape in card, using the template on page 92, for each cracker, cutting out the diamonds where the cracker gathers with a craft knife and making three openings along one side to correspond with the position of the tabs along the other side. With the card flat, decorate as required with contrasting bands of foil, card stars and braid glued in place. Turn the shape over to the wrong side and place a cracker snap onto it, running from one end of the cracker to the other and glue one of the ends of the cracker snap in place.

Roll the card to form the cracker, slotting the tabs into their corre-

ABOVE: A sparkling jewel on a star rosette adds the finishing touch to a cracker made from metallic card with pleated ribbon tied around the ends with decorative braid.

sponding openings. Gather in one of the cut out areas with ribbon tied in a bow. Fill the cracker with a gift and sweets then tie ribbon around the other end of it, securing it with a bow. Glue the loose end of the cracker snap in place inside the end of the tube.

LEFT: Copper-coloured organdie ribbon gathers in the cracker ends with a fan made of pleated gold foil providing decoration, simply held in place with a metal paper fastener.

CHRISTMAS GIFTS

Giving and receiving gifts is an intrinsic part of the Christmas ritual celebrated all around the world and is one of the most enjoyable aspects of the festivities.

Gift giving is in fact the oldest of all the midwinter customs. Ten thousand years ago, when the peoples of the ancient world celebrated the Winter Solstice to mark that the worst of the winter was over and that Spring was on its way, gifts of food were exchanged so that the feasting involved would be as varied and lavish as possible. It was at the festival of Kalends, the celebration of the New Year in ancient Rome, that present giving first became popular. Originally gifts of evergreen branches from the grove of the goddess Strenia were given, then later "honeyed things, that the year of the recipient might be full of sweetness, lamps, that it might be full of light, silver, gold and precious metals, that wealth might flow in".

But the custom took on a renewed significance with the celebration of the birth of Christ. At Christmastime gifts are exchanged to mark the birth of Jesus, just as the three kings brought their gifts to him of gold, frankincense and myrrh. In the same way as the gifts given by the ancient Romans were imbued with significance, each year when we exchange our gifts we give with them our hope that friends and relatives be endowed with all good things in the year ahead.

For children of different countries, the excitement of the custom is surrounded by particular legends of mysterious giftbringers: Father Christmas, St Nicholas, Santa Claus, Mother Star, La Befana, The Christchild and others, who bring gifts in the night from places far away, rewarding and approving the children.

The meaning behind the giving of gifts has perhaps become overshadowed in more recent years by commercial pressures, but the enjoyment the custom brings is still as strong as ever. Making your own home-made gifts revives some of the original sentiments the custom contains, and the time and thought involved is sure to be appreciated by the friends and family members who receive them.

Many of the gift ideas shown over the following pages can be made ahead of time and some of the food gifts will benefit from a short storage period to allow the flavours to mature. An evening set aside to make presents is satisfying as well as productive; one batch of chutney or cookies will yield enough to make gifts for several people.

FOOD GIFTS

Food gifts make impressive presents and can be prepared in batches ahead of time. It is worth saving unusually shaped bottles and jars, then fill them with delicious chutneys and preserves, flavoured oils and vinegars. Circles cut from oddments of rich shimmering fabrics make exquisite tops for the jars especially when tied in place with gold cords and tassels. Labels made from metallic card and written with gold and silver pens give a professional finish.

ABOVE: Pear preserve makes an ideal last-minute gift and all the ingredients are easy to find. The delicious fruit preserve is a medley of pears and pineapple with lime and lemon. A cinnamon stick or two is placed in each jar when the preserve is potted.

CRANBERRY CHUTNEY

450 g (1 lb) fresh or frozen cranberries
450 g (1 lb) eating apples, peeled, cored
and roughly chopped
finely grated rind and juice of 1 orange
175 g (6 oz) sultanas
10 ml (2 tsp) mild chilli seasoning
150 ml (¹/₄ pint) wine vinegar
150 ml (¹/₄ pint) malt vinegar
5 ml (1 tsp) salt
225 g (8 oz) sugar

Place the cranberries in a preserving pan with the apples, orange rind and juice, sultanas, chilli, wine vinegar and salt. Simmer for about 15 minutes or until the fruit is soft. Add the malt vinegar and sugar and boil slowly until thick. Pot in the usual way. Mature for one month

MAKES ABOUT 1.4 KG (3 LB).

Chutneys and Preserves
CRANBERRY CHUTNEY
PEAR PRESERVE
LIME CURD

Cookies and Truffles
SWEDISH SPICE BISCUITS
LEBKUCHEN
CHOCOLATE TRUFFLES

Flavoured Vinegars and Oils
HERB VINEGAR
WHOLE HEADS OF GARLIC IN
OLIVE OIL
ROSEMARY AND LIME VINEGAR
LAYERED OLIVES IN HERB AND
SPICE OIL

Fruits and Spirits
PRUNES IN RUM
DRIED FIGS IN BRANDY
ORANGE AND JUNIPER GIN
CHRISTMAS VODKA LIQUEUR

PEAR PRESERVE

1.4 kg (3 lb) ripe pears
350 g (12 oz) fresh prepared pineapple
2 cinnamon sticks
finely grated rind and juice of 1 lime
finely grated rind and juice of 1 lemon
1.1 kg (2¹/₂ lb) sugar
175 g (6 oz) chopped walnuts (optional)

Peel, core and finely chop the pears. Chop the pineapple. Place in

a preserving pan with the cinnamon and simmer for 45 minutes until soft. Stir in the citrus rind and juice, and the sugar.

Lower the heat and simmer gently for about 30 minutes or until setting point is reached. If adding walnuts, cool for 20 minutes before adding. Pot in the usual way, placing a cinnamon stick or two in each pot if liked.

MAKES ABOUT 2.7 KG (6 LB).

LIME CURD

225 g (8 oz) caster sugar
4 eggs
finely grated rind of 2 limes
juice of 4 limes
125 g (4 oz) unsalted butter, cubed
pinch of salt

Whisk the sugar and eggs together until pale and creamy. Add the lime rind, juice and butter. Cook in a double boiler, stirring occasionally, for about 30 minutes or until holding a ribbon trail. Alternatively, if you are brave, stir constantly over a gentle heat, but do not boil, until thickened. Pot in the usual way. Eat within 1 month.

MAKES ABOUT 900 G (2 LB).

LEFT: Clockwise from far left, a gift selection of cranberry chutney, pear preserve and lime curd, potted and ready to be topped with decorative lids and labels. The chutney can be made ahead of time as it benefits from being stored for a month for the flavours to mature, but if left until the last minute then include instructions for maturing on the label. The lime curd has a limited life, so pot into small jars and include an 'eat by' date on the tag.

ABOVE: One batch of Swedish spice biscuits will make enough for several gift packages. Choose shaped cutters to make them extra special. When they are ready for wrapping, make them into simple bundles, using large squares of clear cellophane, and tie them with ribbon.

SWEDISH SPICE BISCUITS

200 g (7 oz) unsalted butter
200 g (7 oz) caster sugar
2 eggs
500-550 g (1-1¼ lbs) plain white flour
2.5 ml (½ tsp) cinnamon
2.5 ml (½ tsp) ground cardamom
5 ml (1 tsp) cream of tartar
2.5 ml (½ tsp) bitter almond essence
beaten egg, to glaze
crushed sugar lumps, chopped nuts, and icing sugar, to decorate

Cream the butter and sugar together. Beat in the eggs. Divide the mixture in two. In one bowl, beat in half the flour sifted with the spices and cream of tartar. In the other, beat in the remaining flour and the almond essence. Wrap and chill for 15 minutes.

Roll out each mixture thinly and cut out decorative shapes. Place on a baking sheet and glaze with beaten egg. Sprinkle with the crushed sugar or chopped nuts, or decorate when baked with icing sugar sifted over paper stencils. Bake at 200°C (400°F) Gas mark 6 for about 6 minutes. Leave for 5 minutes to cool on the baking sheet then transfer to a wire rack to cool completely. Store in an airtight tin for up to 3 weeks.

MAKES ABOUT 70.

LEBKUCHEN

These little Christmas biscuits are made in German-speaking countries. The finest were reported to come from Nuremberg in the 14th century where they were a great delicacy. They can be hung on the tree as decorations.

3 egg whites
200 g (7 oz) icing sugar, sifted
5 ml (1 tsp) mixed spice
175 g (6 oz) unblanched almonds, coarsely ground
50 g (2 oz) plain chocolate, grated
50 g (2 oz) chopped candied peel
30 ice-cream wafers or about 8 sheets rice paper

FOR THE ICING :
50 g (2 oz) plain chocolate, grated
50 g (2 oz) icing sugar, sifted

Whisk the egg whites until firm. Gradually whisk in the icing sugar and spice until the meringue is stiff and glossy. Fold in the almonds, chocolate and candied peel.

Cut the wafers or rice paper into decorative shapes. Neatly mound a little meringue on each one about 1.5cm (¼ inch) high, tapering it to the edges. Transfer to a baking sheet to dry for several

hours or overnight. Bake at 180°C (350°F) Gas mark 4 for about 25 minutes or until beginning to colour at the edges.

Meanwhile, make the icing. Melt the chocolate with 30 ml (2 tbsp) water. Stir the icing sugar into 15 ml (1 tbsp) hot water. Mix

with the chocolate and cover with a damp cloth.

Cool the biscuits slightly then dip the tops into the icing. The heat will set the icing. These will keep for several weeks in an airtight tin.

MAKES ABOUT 60.

CHOCOLATE TRUFFLES

275 g (10 oz) plain dark chocolate
50 g (2 oz) unsalted butter, cubed
300 ml ($^{1}/_{2}$ pint) double cream or crème fraîche
45 ml (3 tbsp) orange liqueur, dark rum or brandy

FOR THE COATING:
450g (1 lb) plain dark chocolate
edible gold leaf, to decorate

Melt the chocolate, butter and cream together over a gentle heat. The mixture should only be tepid. Stir – over-mixing will make the mixture grainy. Stir in the liqueur. Pour into a shallow tray and refrigerate until firm. Roll teaspoonfuls of mixture into smooth balls and chill. Melt the remaining chocolate and pour a little onto a plate. Carefully roll each truffle in the chocolate to give a rough texture on the outside. Chill until set.

Gently apply small bits of gold leaf to each truffle by rolling over the sheet of gold leaf very gently. Transfer to paper cases and store in an airtight container in the refrigerator for up to 2 weeks or freeze them for up to 3 months.

MAKES ABOUT 30.

LEFT: Far left, Swedish spice biscuits decorated with chopped nuts and icing sugar stencilled stars. Centre, the chocolate truffles can be gilded with edible gold leaf for an opulent treat. Right, heart- and crescent-shaped lebkuchen.

ABOVE: For whole heads of garlic in oil choose the freshest garlic you can find. The heads are roasted in the oven, wrapped in foil to release their pungent aroma, before being submerged in olive oil.

WHOLE HEADS OF GARLIC IN OLIVE OIL

4 very large heads of fresh garlic
sprigs of fresh herbs
about 600 ml (1 pint) good olive oil

Peel the outer layers from the garlic to expose a head of cloves. Loosely wrap the garlic in an oiled foil parcel and bake at 190°C (375°F) Gas mark 5 for 20 minutes or until tender but not disintegrating.

Place each head of garlic in one of four jars into which it will fit snugly. Tuck sprigs of herbs around the garlic and pour over olive oil to cover. Seal tightly. Store for 2 months before using to allow the flavours to develop.

ROSEMARY AND LIME VINEGAR

1 litre (13/4 pints) white wine vinegar
sprigs of fresh rosemary
2-3 garlic cloves, peeled and sliced
1 lime, quartered or sliced

Place the vinegar in a non-corrosive saucepan and add 4 large sprigs of rosemary. Slowly bring to the boil, boil for 1 minute then leave overnight to infuse. Place fresh sprigs of rosemary, slices of lime and garlic into sterilized bottles. Strain over the vinegar and seal. Store in a cool dry place for at least 2 weeks to mature. Keeps for at least 6 months.

MAKES 1 LITRE (13/4 PINTS).

HERB VINEGAR

Use any combination of fresh herbs that appeal.

4 sprigs fresh tarragon
4 sprigs fresh rosemary
4 sprigs fresh thyme
2 garlic cloves, peeled and sliced
1.1 litres (2 pints) white wine vinegar

Place a sprig of each herb and a couple of slices of garlic in sterilized decorative bottles. Top up with vinegar and seal. Store in a cool dry place for 2 weeks before using. Keeps for at least 6 months.

MAKES 1.1 LITRES (2 PINTS).

LAYERED OLIVES IN HERB AND SPICE OIL

450 g (1 lb) mixed olives of your choice (plain or stuffed, black or green)
coriander seeds
thin slices of lemon and lime
sprigs of fresh herbs
olive oil

Place one third of the olives in a layer on the bottom of a decorative 750ml (1¼ pint) jar. Sprinkle with coriander seeds and cover with a layer of lemon slices. Tuck a herb sprig down the side.

Cover with half the remaining olives. Cover these in turn with a layer of lime slices and finish with a layer of the remaining olives. Pour over olive oil to cover then seal tightly. Change the layers according to availability of produce.

LEFT: From left to right, Layered olives in herb and spice oil, whole heads of garlic in olive oil, herb vinegar and rosemary and lime vinegar. As the flavoured vinegars and oils have a long shelf life and need to be left for some time before use to allow the flavours to develop and mature, they can all be made well in advance of the Christmas celebrations. For those not so well organised, make them nearer the festivities but don't forget to include the storing and maturing advice on an attractive label.

PRUNES IN RUM

In France, Agen prunes are traditionally soaked in Armagnac. Here rum provides a seasonal variation.

450 g (1 lb) large prunes
about 600 ml (1 pint) dark rum
225 g (8 oz) caster sugar

Place the prunes in a clean jar. Stir the rum and sugar together until dissolved and pour over the fruit to cover. Seal and leave to mature for at least 2 months before using.

DRIED FIGS IN BRANDY

450 g (1 lb) dried figs
1 vanilla pod, split
about 600 ml (1 pint) brandy
225 g (8 oz) caster sugar

Place the figs and vanilla pod in a clean jar. Stir the brandy and sugar together until dissolved and pour over the fruit to cover. Seal and leave to mature for at least 2 months before using.

ORANGE & JUNIPER GIN

10 oranges
2 cloves
4 juniper berries, crushed
750 ml (1 1/4 pints) gin
225 g (8 oz) sugar

Peel the oranges neatly and dry the peel in a low oven for several hours or until dry and brittle. Put the orange peel in a wide-necked jar with the cloves, juniper berries and gin. Seal and leave in a cool dark place for about 6 weeks, shaking occasionally.

Dissolve the sugar in 300ml (1/2 pint) water and boil for 3 minutes. Cool. Strain the gin and stir in the syrup. Strain through a fine sieve into bottles and seal. Store for 2 months before using.

MAKES ABOUT 1.1 LITRES (2 PINTS).

LEFT: For orange and juniper gin the peel is removed from the oranges and dried slowly in a low oven until dry. The flavour from the peel can then be left to permeate into the gin along with other spicy additions before the spirit is decanted into bottles.

CHRISTMAS VODKA LIQUEUR

Use organic, unwaxed fruit for the best flavour.

1 orange, stuck with cloves
2 clementines, pierced several times
about 6 fresh clementine leaves
(optional)
pared rind of 1 lemon or lime
2 x 5 cm (2in) cinnamon sticks
10 ml (2 tsp) coriander seeds
1 vanilla pod, split
6 cardamom pods, split
sprig of rosemary
45 ml (3 tbsp) sugar
200 ml (7 fl oz) dry white wine
750 ml (1¹/₄ pints) vodka

Place all the ingredients in a wide jar and top up with the wine and vodka to cover. Seal and leave in a cool dark place, shaking occasionally, for about 6 weeks. Strain through a fine sieve to serve.

MAKES 1.1 LITRES (2 PINTS).

LEFT: Clockwise from back left, orange and juniper gin, prunes in rum, Christmas vodka liqueur and dried figs in brandy. A fruity tipple is always well received at Christmas and these spirits laced with sweet spices and packed with plump fruits make the most luxurious gifts.

POMANDERS, CUSHIONS & SCENTED SACHETS

Pomanders, scented sachets and cushions make perfect presents and fill the air with their festive aroma of rich spices. Made with loops of ribbon, pomanders can be hung in a wardrobe or linen cupboard and are said to repel moths. To make them, choose thin-skinned citrus fruits, such as oranges, lemons and limes or thick-skinned green apples and stud them with cloves. Scented sachets and cushions made from scraps of silk or taffeta fabric can be decorated with woven metallic ribbons and braids for really exquisite results. Choose pot pourri with a fine texture to fill them.

RIGHT: Pomanders made from oranges and limes studded with cloves need to be left to cure in a spice mixture for several weeks until dry. Powdered orris root is added to the mixture and acts as a fixative for the wonderful spice-rich aroma.

POMANDERS

You will need: whole fruits, 25 g (1 oz) of whole large-headed cloves for each fruit, a bodkin or fine knitting needle, ribbon or braid, tape, and for enough spice mixture to cure several pomanders; 25 g (1 oz) powdered orris root, 50 g (2 oz) ground cinnamon, 25 g (1 oz) of powdered cloves and 10 g (½ oz) allspice.

Begin by marking out a band around the fruit which will be left free of cloves for the ribbon. Do this by sticking a cross of 1.2 cm (½ in) wide tape around the fruit.

Stick the cloves into the fruit,

either at random or in a pattern of lines, using the bodkin to make holes in the skin, until the areas between the channels are completely covered. The pomander will shrink as it dries, so position the cloves close together but with spaces between; a clove's head apart is a good guide.

Mix the curing spices together in a shallow bowl and turn the studded fruits in the mixture so they are completely covered with the powder. Leave the bowl of pomanders in a dry, airy place, turning them over in the spices every day. Drying the pomanders can take from 4-10

weeks depending on the size of the fruit and the atmosphere of the room. The dried fruits will sound hollow when they are tapped and will be smaller and darker in colour. Wrap a length of braid or ribbon around each pomander and tie in a bow or a loop to complete.

SCENTED SACHET

You will need: a rectangle of fabric 13 cm x 44 cm (5 in x 17½ in), pot pourri, ribbons, and braids, sewing thread, woven metallic ribbon (optional).

Stitch bands of woven metallic ribbon across the right side of the fabric strip to embellish the fabric if required, bearing in mind when positioning them that the top edge of the finished sachet will be 9 cm (3½ in) in from both short ends. Fold the strip of fabric in half lengthways, with the right side together and stitch down both sides, leaving the top open and taking a 1.5 cm (5/8 in) seam allowance.

Trim the seams and press them open, then turn to the right side. Turn the top 9 cm (3½ in) inside the sachet and press the folded edge flat. Fill two-thirds full with pot pourri then gather in just above the filling and tie it together with a length of braid or ribbon, tied in a bow.

SCENTED CUSHION

You will need: a strip of fabric; for the square cushion 17 cm x 37 cm (6¾ in x 14½ in), or for the rectangular cushion 18 cm x 49 cm (7 in x 19¼ in), a piece of thin calico; for the square cushion 17 cm x 31 cm (6¾ in x 12¼ in) or for the rectangular cushion 18 cm by 43 cm (7 in x 17 in), pot pourri, 4 small buttons, sewing thread, tasselled braid or cord, braid and woven metallic ribbon (optional).

Decorate the right side of the fabric with a strip of woven metallic ribbon sewn lengthways to the fabric, covering the edges with braid, if required. Turn under 1 cm (½ in), then a further 2 cm (¾ in) to the wrong side along one short edge of the fabric strip, press and stitch in place, then make 4 buttonholes along this edge, one 3 cm (1¼ in) in from each side and the other two spaced evenly between them. Turn under 1 cm (½ in) along the other short edge and stitch down, then make a line of tacking stitches, across the strip, 5 cm (2 in) from this edge.

Lay the strip flat, with the right side facing you and the buttonhole edge to your right, fold the edge with the buttonholes over to the left to meet the tacked line, then fold the left-hand edge of fabric over to the right, folding along the line of tacking. Pin then stitch down both sides, taking 1.5 cm (⅝ in) seam allowances. Trim the seams, turn the cushion to the right side and press flat. Stitch the buttons in place and sew tasselled braid or cord around the edge of the cushion or decorate with ribbon.

LEFT: Scented cushions, embellished with sumptuous braids and metallic ribbon, are surrounded by scented sachets and pomanders. Pot pourri full of large pieces of pods and seedheads would make the cushions and sachets look too lumpy so use a filling with a fine texture.

To make the bag that will contain the pot pourri inside the cushion, fold the strip of calico fabric in half, with right sides together. Stitch around the 3 sides, taking seam allowances as before and leaving a gap in one of them for filling. Trim the seam and turn to the right side. Fill with pot pourri then stitch the hole closed. Place the bag of pot pourri inside the cushion and fasten the buttons.

STATIONERY FOLDER & FRAMES

ABOVE: The frame can be custom made to fit the dimensions of any picture.

RIGHT: The stationery folder is made from a single shaped piece of card. You could include a feather quill pen and a stick of gold sealing wax in the folder.

The stationery folder and picture frames can be made from the simplest materials which, if chosen with care, make really sumptuous Christmas gifts that anyone would be glad to receive. Choose oddments of moire or fine jacquard fabrics to cover them and add gold cord and rosettes for the finishing touch.

STATIONERY FOLDER

You will need: a piece of thin card 40 cm x 50 cm (15¾ in x 19¾ in), a piece of fabric and a piece of lining fabric the same size, spray adhesive, a length of cord and ribbon, 120 cm (48 in) of 2 cm (¾ in) wide metallic ribbon, a craft knife, A5 size 14.8 cm x 21 cm (5¾ in x 8¼ in) writing paper and matching envelopes.

Draw the shape onto the card following the template given on page 93 and cut it out with a craft knife. Score all the lines as shown except the inside fold, using a pointed implement, on one side of the card (this will be the outside of the folder). Score the inside fold on the other side of the card and then crease all the folds. Glue the fabric to the outside of the folder with spray adhesive, folding the card whilst smoothing the fabric over it.

Turn it over to the wrong side, cut the excess fabric from around the card and cut the line that runs between the side flap and the base as shown on the template. Glue the lining fabric to the inside of the folder in the same way as before and cut away the excess.

Cut the ribbon into lengths to fit along each of the edges that form the top edge and the sides, from the base to inside fold as shown, then glue the pieces in place with it overlapping the folder's edges by 1 cm (⅜ in). When the glue is dry,

turn the folder over to the wrong side and glue the ribbon down so that it binds the edges.

With the front and side flaps inside, fold to form the folder, pushing the base flap inside. Roll the writing paper in half, place it onto the envelopes and tie a piece of ribbon around them. Put them into the folder, bend the top of the folder over and tie the cord around it to complete.

FABRIC-COVERED FRAMES

The frame can be made to fit any size of postcard or photograph and will measure 2 cm (¾ in) bigger all round than the picture when complete.
You will need: a piece of medium-weight card, fabric, a small piece of fine iron-on interfacing, a craft knife, spray adhesive, metal paper fasteners, a bradawl, rosettes or buttons, glue (optional).

Measure the dimensions of the picture and draw its outline onto the card. Draw a line around this outline to make a 2 cm (¾ in) border and mark the fold lines, then another line to make a border 3 cm (1¼ in) bigger than the first one. Cut along the outer line with a craft knife.

Draw a square at each corner between the edges and the inner

LEFT: The frames can be made to fit pictures of all shapes and sizes and are covered with fabric oddments. We used richly patterned woven fabrics that particularly suited the style of the images. The stationery folder holds a bundle of writing paper and envelopes.

border lines and cut them away to leave a flap on each side of the frame. Round off the ends of the top and bottom flaps and cut the ends of the side flaps straight, slanting slightly inwards. Score the folds on the outside and bend in the flaps.

Cut the fabric 1 cm (½ in) bigger all round than the card and iron a piece of interfacing to correspond with each of the flap ends on the wrong side of the fabric to prevent it fraying. Stick the fabric over the back and sides of the frame using spray adhesive, bending in the flaps as the fabric is smoothed into place. Snip the excess fabric on the curves and corners, then fold the fabric over to the wrong side of the

card, and glue in place.

To keep the frame upright, cut out a support in card measuring two-thirds of the height of the frame by 7 cm (2¾ in) wide, then cut the sides so they slope in from 7 cm to 4 cm (1½ in) at the other end. Score a line 1 cm (½ in), parallel to the narrow end and bend along the line, to make a fixing strip. Join the support to the back of the frame, with paper fasteners pushed through two holes made through the strip and frame back with a bradawl.

Cut out another piece of card, 2 cm (¾ in) bigger all round than the picture, to provide a backing for it and to strengthen the frame, and

put it in place. Bend over the side flaps first, followed by top and bottom flaps and make holes, using the bradawl, through all thicknesses of card and fabric, 1.8 cm (5/8 in) from the frame's outer edge, one at each corner with holes spaced evenly between them along the sides.

Fix the sides and bottom flaps down with paper fasteners pushed through the holes to the back of the frame. Slide the picture in from the top, then fasten the last flap down. Decorate the heads of the paper fasteners with small ornamental mouldings like the painted plastic rosettes shown in the picture, or with buttons or flat beads if required, sticking them on with glue.

RAG DOLL

A rag doll makes an enchanting gift for a child. The stunning ballgown is made from scraps of sparkling fabrics, decorated with beads and sequins.

You will need: a piece of calico 50 cm x 40 cm (19½ in x 16 in), kapok filling, bouclé wool for the hair, embroidery threads for the face details, a piece of net 90 cm x 25 cm (36 in x 10 in) for the underskirt and a piece of fabric the same size for the dress skirt, a scrap of contrasting fabric for the bodice, a piece of woven metallic ribbon 36 cm (14 in) long for the stole and 2 gold tassels, a selection of ribbons, braids and beads, 3 press studs, scissors and sewing threads.

Draw the shape of the doll shown as a template on page 95 on to paper to make a pattern, and cut out 2 pieces in calico. Pin the fabric pieces together and stitch around the edges, taking a seam allowance of 6 mm (¼ in) and leaving a 4 cm (1½ in) opening down one side. Trim the seam, clipping the curves, then turn right side out. Fill the body firmly with kapok and hand stitch closed the side opening.

Starting at the back of the neck, coil the bouclé wool around the head, following the hairline, and hand stitch it in place as you go, working round and round until the area inside the hairline is all filled in. For a fringe, make a row of small loops with the wool and lay them along the top of the head, stitching over the strands to hold them in place, then cut the loops. For the rest of the hair, make larger loops and, working each side separately, stitch the strands in place along the centre top of the head. Cut the loops open and trim the hair into an even shape, then embroider the face details.

To make the underskirt pattern, draw a 21 cm (8½ in) diameter semicircle with a smaller semicircle 5.5 cm (2½ in) in diameter cut out of it, then add 1 cm (½ in) seam allowance along the straight edges. Cut 2 pieces in net and stitch them together along the straight edges, leaving a 4 cm (1½ in) opening at

the waist end of one of the seams. Cut a length of narrow ribbon to fit the doll's waist measurement plus 1 cm (½ in), then gather the under-skirt waist with running stitches, to fit the doll and stitch the ribbon over the gathers so the extra ribbon sticks out at one side. Sew on a press stud fastener at the waist.

Cut 2 pieces for the dress skirt and join the side seams in the same way as the underskirt. Bind the hem with contrasting bias binding. Cut 2 bodice pieces, shown as a template on page 95, in a contrast-ing fabric. With right sides togeth-er, pin together and stitch, leaving the waist edge open and taking a 6 mm (¼ in) seam. Trim the seam, clip the curves and turn right side out, then press flat. Gather the skirt waist to fit the bodice and with right sides together, pin the bodice to it and stitch. Sew 2 press stud fasteners to the side of the bodice and make shoulder straps out of narrow ribbon and stitch them in place on the bodice.

To make the stole, gather the ends of the woven metallic ribbon and sew on 2 tassels. For the slip-pers, cut 2 pieces out of 2.5 cm (1 in) wide ribbon for each slipper, shown as the shaded area on the template, stitch them together, trim the seam and turn right side out. Stitch flat braid around the top and attach fine gold cords at each side of the slippers, to cross around the legs and tie in bows.

Make a crown out of gold cord to fit around the head and decorate with a star bead. Sew small beads on to make earings and a row of sequins to make a necklace.

COVERED BOXES

Fabric- and wallpaper-covered boxes make attractive and useful Christmas gifts in their own right or are ideal way to package other gifts. The hat box uses wallpaper as part of the construction, so the pattern choices are infinite. Add a tasselled cord and line the box with gold tissue paper for a really luxurious finish.

ABOVE: A shoe box is transformed when it is covered with a beautiful fabric and given a contrasting lining.
FAR RIGHT: A taffeta ribbon bow provides an extravagant flourish to complete the shoe box.

RIGHT: All the pieces are gathered together ready to assemble the hat box.

THE HAT BOX

The finished box measures 36 cm (14 in) in diameter and 16 cm (6¼ in) deep, but you can make the box in other sizes.

You will need: a circle of heavy-weight card 36 cm (14 in) in diameter for the base and another circle

36.5 cm (14¼ in) in diameter for the lid, 2 strips of medium-weight card 15.5 cm x 63.5 cm (6 in x 25 in) for the sides and 2 more 4 cm x 63.5 cm (1½ in x 25 in) for the lid bands, a craft knife, wallpaper, wallpaper paste, glue, clothes pegs, a star stencil, gold spray paint.

Join the 2 side strips together with glue, overlapping the short ends by 12 cm (4½ in) and holding them together with clothes pegs until the glue is dry. Join the lid bands in the same way. Cut a strip of wallpaper to fit the side band with a border of 2.5 cm (1 in) extra allowed along the base edge, then paste it to one side of the card. Cover the lid band with wallpaper in the same way, leaving the border along the lid edge.

Roll the side band around the base circle and glue the overlapping ends together, using clothes pegs to hold them together until the glue is completely dry. Snip the border at 2 cm (¾ in) intervals to make flaps all along the base edge, push the circle down to meet the edge of the card and stick all the flaps to the the base's underside. Cut a circle of wallpaper the same size as the base and stick it to its underside.

Join the lid of the box and cover in the same way, finishing by sticking the circle of wallpaper to the top of the lid. Stencil a gold star in the centre of the lid and a row of them around the side of the box.

FABRIC-COVERED SHOE BOXES

You will need: a shoe box, a piece of fabric approximately 70 cm x 100 cm (27½ in x 39 in) and a piece of lining fabric approximately 40 cm x 80 cm (16 in x 31½ in), spray adhesive, scissors, a length of ribbon.

Place the base of the box on the wrong side of the fabric, mark the corner points and positions of the side flaps by drawing lines on the fabric to make a right angle from each corner. Measure the depth of the box, add 2 cm (¾ in) to this measurement, then mark the total measurement on the side flaps. Add 0.5 cm (¼ in) allowance all round for turnings, then, having marked the fabric, cut it out.

Snip the allowance diagonally

into each corner point. Turn the allowance to the wrong side at the ends of the side flaps, leaving the allowance on the end flaps flat. Press with an iron then glue them down. Spray adhesive on to the wrong side of the fabric and stick the box between the corner points, turning the box over and smoothing the fabric over its base.

Smooth the end flaps in place over the box, so the turnings go round the sides of the box. Snip the turnings at the top corner points

and smooth the flaps down to the inside of the box. Smooth the side flaps over the box to the inside with the folded edges overlapping the allowance on the end flaps.

Measure the fabric for the lid in the same way but make the depth of the flaps twice the depth of the lid plus 1 cm ($\frac{1}{2}$ in). Stick the fabric in place following the same order as before.

To make the lining for inside the box, measure the fabric in the same way as the outside fabric but make

the flaps 1 cm ($\frac{1}{2}$ in) shorter than the depth of the box. Add an allowance for turnings of 5 mm ($\frac{1}{4}$ in) on all edges and turn and press all of them down except the end flap sides. Cut out the fabric and stick to the inside of the box, beginning with the base, then the end flaps and finally the side flaps. Cut out a piece of lining fabric the same size as the lid, turn under and press 5 mm ($\frac{1}{4}$ in) on all four edges, then stick it centrally inside the lid. Decorate the lid with a bow if required.

LEFT: A hat box decorated with stencilled gold stars and shoe boxes topped with taffeta bows are good looking as well as practical gifts. Whoever receives these useful storage boxes will want to keep them out on show.

CHRISTMAS STOCKINGS

ABOVE: The stockings can be decorated as simply or as elaborately as you wish. Rows of buttons and braid can be sewn along the cuff or a single rosette and tassel stitched in place.

RIGHT: A Christmas stocking filled to overflowing with goodies awaits discovery at the foot of the bed.

For many children, a stocking filled to the brim with small gifts discovered at the foot of the bed on Christmas morning is one of the most exciting and memorable parts of the festive celebrations. The custom goes back to the fourth century and is thought to have originated from a story of St Nicholas, the man on whom the character of Santa Claus is based. As bishop of Myra in what is now south-west Turkey, he used his own considerable wealth to help the poor, and earned himself saintly status in the process. On one occasion, a nobleman who had fallen on hard times was unable to provide dowries for his three daughters, so one night Bishop Nicholas threw a bag of coins for each of them through the front door of their home which miraculously landed in stockings that were hanging up drying in front of the fire.

Before going to bed on Christmas Eve, children in eager anticipation hang empty stockings on the mantelpiece ready for Santa Claus to fill while they are asleep, and a mince pie and a glass of sherry is left out as refreshment for him. In the 19th century, everyday stockings were more ornately decorated for this purpose with the addition of braids, fringes and embroidery and towards the end of the century mothers made special stockings in needlepoint. Following

on that tradition, home-made stockings are easy to make, using oddments of fabric, trimmed with tassels and rosettes.

THE BASIC STOCKING

You will need: a piece of fabric 70 cm x 55 cm (28 in x 20 in) and another piece the same size in a contrasting fabric for the lining (allow more fabric for larger patterns); pins, needle and sewing thread; paper.

Draw the stocking on to paper to make a pattern, following the template given on page 94. Allowances of 1.5 cm (5/8 in) are included for all the seams. Fold the fabrics in half lengthways and cut out a pair of stocking shapes in the main fabric and another pair in the

lining, then cut a rectangle of main fabric 6.5 cm x 19 cm (2½ in x 7 5/8 in) from the main fabric left-overs to make a hanging loop.

With the right sides together, pin the two main stocking shapes together and stitch around the outer edge, leaving the top open. Trim the seam to 6 mm (¼ in) and snip the curved parts of the seam allowance close to the stitching. Turn it to the right side and press the seam edges flat. Turn the top edge seam allowance to the inside of the stocking and press.

Make the lining in the same way but leave it with the wrong sides facing you. Turn the top edge seam allowance over to the outside and press.

To make the hanging loop, fold the fabric in half lengthways, with right sides together and stitch down the long edge. Trim the seam, turn it to the right side and press flat. Fold it in half and stitch in place.

Push the lining into the stocking, pinning the folded edges together around the top and slip stitch them together. Finish off the top with cord, hand stitched in place.

STOCKINGS WITH CUFF

You will need: the same materials as for the basic stocking plus an extra piece of a contrasting fabric 55 cm x 40 cm (22 in x 16 in) to make the cuff of the stocking.

Cut out the stocking shapes in

the main fabric and another pair in lining and stitch them together as before, but leave the top edges unfolded. Push the lining into the stocking, and tack the edges together around the top. Make the hanging loop as before and tack it to the inside top of the stocking so the loop points down into the stocking.

Make a pattern for the cuff using the template then fold the fabric in half and cut out two pairs of cuff shapes. Take one of these pairs and with right sides together, stitch down both side edges to make a tube. Press the seams open.

Join the other pair in the same way then turn one of the tubes to the right side and push it inside the other, matching the seams and pinning the bottom edges together. Stitch along this edge then turn the cuff to the right side, folding along the seam and bringing the raw edges together.

Push the cuff inside the stocking, and stitch them together around the top. Fold the cuff to the right side of the stocking and press. Finish off the stocking with tasselled braid or a rosette in a contrasting colour.

ABOVE LEFT: Stockings with tasselled cuff and rosette decoration hanging from the mantelpiece echo the source of the custom; Bishop Nicholas reputedly threw bags of coins into stockings that were hanging to dry by the fire.

ABOVE: As well as small toys and sweets, the filling for a traditional stocking should include an apple at the toe to symbolize good health and a real coin for future wealth; a bag of chocolate money is a reminder of the custom's origin; whilst an orange and some nuts, which were once rare and costly treats, are also essential ingredients.

GIFT WRAPPING

RIGHT: Oddments and waste pieces of card and decorative papers can be used to make your presents look quite distinctive. Try using bands of paper cut-offs in contrasting colours and textures to make your wrapping extra special and finish them off with ribbon, raffia and rosettes.

It only takes a little extra care when wrapping your gifts to make each one look really special. Taking the trouble to wrap a gift prettily shows that you hope the person who receives it will enjoy opening the package as much as the present it contains. Don't wrap them so securely that it makes them difficult to undo, especially for children's gifts. When using sticky tape, turn under one end on each piece to make small tabs that are easy to pull apart.

BAUBLES AND ROSETTE WRAPPINGS

The wrappings for this group of presents combines patterned papers with plains, and a mixture of textures. A band of metallic foil is wound around a parcel wrapped in a hand-printed Indian paper with a deep red and gold design, then a wide organdie ribbon in shimmering bronze is tied around it to make a sumptuous bow, finished off with a gold star bead.

Raffia can be used in a decorative way to tie up packages, using lots of lengths of it, all together. Look out for natural raffia, dyed in lovely rich colours and sold in long hanks. We used pink raffia, tied over green foil, and added two small frosted glass baubles, to give the parcel sparkle and make unusual name tags. Greetings can be written on them with metallic felt tip

FILIGREE WRAPPINGS

Using doilies as part of the wrapping for your gifts is a quick way to achieve stunning results and they are available in lots of different sizes and patterns. Begin by laying the doilies flat on newspaper and paint them in metallic colours of gold and copper with spray paint.

Larger doilies, big enough to completely cover the gift, can be stuck onto contrasting coloured wrapping paper with spray adhesive, before wrapping the gift in the usual way. Alternatively, add filigree borders to your parcels by overwrapping just the corners or ends of them with the lacy edges of a doilie. Finish them off with glimmering, metallic ribbons.

SEALING WAX

Sealing wax gives a traditional touch to your wrappings. It is an effective way of holding the paper edges together but is also easy and very satisfying to break open. Here, a flat present was enveloped in a stiff marbleized paper, simply folded to form a wallet shape, then a length of flat upholstery braid was tied around it and finished off in a knot. Finally, molten gold sealing wax was dripped onto the braid and left to set, to hold it all in place. Gift tags with cords can be stuck to the parcels with blobs of sealing wax. Traditional red sealing wax suits the festive colour theme but can make packages hard to open, so avoid using it when wrapping gifts for excited children.

FAR LEFT: A flat present can be enveloped to make a simple folder. Here we used a flat braid to provide a stylish tie and a blob of molten gold sealing wax to give it a classical feel.

pen, but you should make sure that presents decorated in this way stay at the top of the pile so the baubles don't get crushed and broken.

To wrap a bottle, we rolled one in gold paper and folded the top over to make it flat and square, sticking it in place with a piece of double-sided tape. A piece of corrugated card was wrapped around it, then a piece of orange foil was wrapped over that, both being taped in place at the back and finished off at the front with a bow of paper ribbon.

Rosettes are easy to make out of paper ribbon. Cut three lengths of the ribbon 10 cm (4 in) long and open them out. Gather each one in evenly across the middle and bunch all three pieces together, winding fine wire around the gathers to hold them together, then fold back each of the ribbon pieces to cover the wire, fanning out the ribbon so the edges of each piece overlaps the next to form the rosette. Glue an anise star painted copper to the middle of the rosette to finish off the centre, then glue it onto the parcel.

LEFT: Paper doilies are easy to find and when sprayed with metallic paint bring a delicate filigree look to your wrappings. Use large doilies to completely cover the parcel or smaller ones to bind around the centre or envelope the corners.

GREETINGS CARDS

years Christmas cards became popularised worldwide. Early cards showed Christmas feasts, plump turkeys and plum puddings, lanterns and robins in the snow; images which are equally popular in the present day.

CHERUBS AND ANGELS

Black and white photocopied images look extremely effective used as cut outs and stuck onto con-trasting paper and card. Cherubs and angels make appropriate images to suit the season and can be found in books of engravings. Choose designs that are self-contained, with an outline that isn't too complicated, then photocopy them and carefully cut them out. Details within the designs can be picked out with gold or silver felt tip pens.

For the cherub card, the motif was glued onto a piece of hand-

ABOVE: Stars and moons greetings cards. The simple motifs cut out of carrot ends can be printed at random on to coloured papers and card. They are fun for children to make as Christmas approaches and, when finished off with tassels and cords, give a charming hand-made finish.

RIGHT: Classical images such as cherubs and angels have been used extensively in black and white engravings. We used them as photocopied motifs and produced distinctive results.

When Henry Cole, a British art enthusiast, was faced with the task of hand writing Christmas greetings to his huge circle of friends he hit upon a new idea and in 1843 he commissioned J.C. Horsley to design the first Christmas card. Printed on stiff cardboard then hand coloured, the image depicted a Victorian family raising their glasses in a toast. The custom of sending seasonal greetings in the form of a card was not instantly taken up and was considered by some to be in bad taste but three years later the cards were produced with a print run of one thousand and cost one shilling each. It was five years before the second design appeared and what was at first thought of as a passing craze was adopted by the Victorians, who loved to send and collect them. Cheaper methods of printing and the introduction of lower postal rates helped the custom to become established and over the next fifty

made paper, using its rough, uneven edge as a feature and folded double. This was placed over a piece of white card folded in half and two holes were punched through all thicknesses at the top and held together with a length of sparkling ribbon, tied in a bow.

For the angel card the design was stuck directly onto folded white card with an interesting texture of silky threads and metallic dots. It was finished off with white and gold knotted cord, in the same way as before. The acanthus leaf design was stuck onto a rectangle of gold card, which was then fixed onto folded black card, to leave a narrow border all around it. A bow of dark green organdie completed the card.

STARS AND MOONS

Carrot printing Christmas cards are fun for children to make. Cut a carrot in half, then cut away the end surfaces of the two pieces to leave a star and moon design. Apply gold paint to the designs with a brush and print them at random onto squares of coloured paper. Mark out borders and add simple dotted motifs around the stars with a gold felt tip pen. Stick the designs on to folded card, leaving narrow borders around the edges. Finish them off with gold cord and tassels as required.

SCENTED STARS

A single star anise decorates a card, adding its own particular fragrance. Paint the stars gold and copper colours to make them sparkle and mount them onto pieces of metallic foil on gold card.

Other spices could be used, such as a few short cinnamon sticks tied to make a bundle on the card with a piece of twine threaded through from the back, or dried bay leaves painted gold glued around the edge of the card to make a border.

ABOVE: Incorporate the sweet scents and spices of the season into your greetings cards. Gilded star anise provide a festive motif as well as adding their own distinctive fragrance. Make sure that you can find envelopes big enough to fit the cards.

CHRISTMAS FOOD

Feasting and festivals go hand in hand and, for most of us, the Christmas feast is the most elaborate meal of the year, involving a great deal of planning and preparation.

During the celebrations, the main meal will usually be served on Christmas Eve or on the day itself, each family following its own traditions, to form the heart of the whole event. In households all over the world, the ingredients that make up this feast might be different but they are always guaranteed to be lavish. The French feast, *le réveillon*, takes place after mass on Christmas Eve, with oysters, champagne and Bûche de Noël. In Finland feasting begins on Christmas Eve after church with roast pork, ham wrapped in rye dough and carrot pudding. In Denmark a Christmas Eve feast is followed on Christmas Day by a cold buffet of pickled herring, caviar, shrimps, meat balls, pâté, smoked leg of lamb, brawn, cold roast pork, smoked sausages and cheeses. Guests may be at the table from noon until late evening. Turkey with traditional stuffing forms the central dish for the British celebration dinner, and is also a favourite in Italy and France, whereas American families, having eaten turkey during Thanksgiving in late November, may sometimes choose an alternative, such as roast beef or ham.

As well as it being a time when family and friends gather to share a Christmas dinner together, there are lots of other goodies that surround the main meal and which have become an essential part of the festivities. Certain cakes and biscuits, for instance, have their own particular significance and superstition attached to them. A popular legend states that you are granted one wish when you take your first bite of mince pie each year and that to eat one mince pie on each of the twelve days of Christmas will bring you good luck in the twelve months ahead, but each of the pies should be eaten in a different house. In Sweden, Denmark, Germany, Norway and Finland some form of Julgröt, porridge or rice pudding, is traditionally served, containing a single almond. Whoever finds the nut in their serving will be lucky, be the first to marry or win a small prize. Many of the traditional sweet delicacies are made from mixtures that include dried fruits, nuts and spices, which were once considered to be rare ingredients but which are now relatively easy to come by.

49

CHRISTMAS DINNERS

RIGHT: Uszka are little stuffed ear-shaped dumplings of boiled dough which can contain a variety of fillings. A Polish traditional filling of mushrooms would be served on Christmas Eve. They are added to the soup just before serving or can be served as an accompaniment to salad or by themselves as hors d'oeuvres.

The main Christmas feast is often the high point of the whole celebrations when all the family come together to enjoy an especially lavish meal of many courses. Whilst the dishes served around the world are quite varied there are also many similarities. Oysters, cured hams and cold meats, salmon, smoked or pickled, stuffed turkey and beef are popular in many countries. The French feast, *le réveillon*, takes place after mass on Christmas Eve, with oysters, foie gras and snails offered as the first course. In Finland feasting begins on Christmas Eve after church with salted salmon and marinaded herring, beetroot salad and baked ham studded with cloves. The recipes that follow are a small selection of dishes enjoyed in countries around the world as part of the Christmas meal.

BARSZCZ Z USZKAMI (Poland)

BRUSSELS SPROUT AND HAZELNUT SOUP (Great Britain)

VARM RÖKT LAX MED SMÖR (Sweden)

DORADE AUX OLIVES (France)

ENSALADA DE NOCHE BUENA (Mexico)

FALSOMAGRO (Italy)

WINTER VEGETABLE GRATIN (Canada)

SCHWEINEROLLBRATEN MIT PFLAUMEN (Germany)

RØDKÅL (Denmark)

BUTTERNUT SQUASH WITH MAPLE SYRUP (USA)

ROAST TURKEY AND STUFFINGS (Great Britain)

POLAND

BARSZCZ Z USZKAMI

BARSZCZ (SOUP)

20 g (3/4 oz) dried mushrooms (cepes)
1 onion, peeled
1 clove
350 g (12 oz) raw beetroot (4-5 small beetroot)
5 ml (1 tsp) wine or raspberry vinegar
5 ml (1 tsp) sugar
100 ml (4 fl oz) medium white wine
cayenne pepper
salt and black pepper
sprigs of parsley and soured cream, to serve

Soak the dried mushrooms in 2 litres (3 pints) water for 30 minutes. Add the onion stuck with the clove, slowly bring to the boil and simmer for 1 hour. Strain the stock (you

should have at least 1½ litres/2½ pints and reserve the mushrooms to make the dumplings.

Trim and peel the beetroot. Simmer in the mushroom stock for about 45 minutes or until very tender. Strain and add the vinegar, sugar, wine and seasoning. Cut the beetroot into julienne strips and add to the soup. Reheat, garnish with parsley and serve with the 'Uszkami' and a bowl of soured cream.

SERVES 6.

USZKAMI (DUMPLINGS)

FOR THE FILLING:
30 g (1 oz) butter
225 g (8 oz) mushrooms, finely chopped
the reserved cooked dried mushrooms, finely chopped
1 small onion, peeled and finely chopped
pinch of cumin
salt and pepper

FOR THE DOUGH:
225 g (8 oz) plain flour
2.5 ml (¹/₂ tsp) salt
1 egg
about 100 ml (4 fl oz) water

Fry the fresh and dried mushrooms with the onion in the butter until well reduced, soft and just beginning to colour. Season to taste with cumin, salt and pepper. Cool.

Mix together the flour, salt, beaten egg and enough water to give a stiff dough. Knead until smooth. Wrap and rest for 15 minutes.

Roll out the dough thinly and stamp into 5 cm (2 in) rounds. Place a little filling in the middle of each one. Dampen the edges and fold over into a crescent shape. Twist into tortellini shapes.

Deep-fry in batches for 2-3 minutes until golden. Serve with the soup immediately or reheat in a hot oven for about 8 minutes.

BRUSSELS SPROUT AND HAZELNUT SOUP

50 g (2 oz) butter
225 g (8 oz) onions, peeled and chopped
1 small potato, peeled and chopped
about 1.1 litres (2 pints) chicken or vegetable stock
2 bay leaves
salt and pepper
450 g (1 lb) Brussels sprouts, trimmed and chopped
125 g (4 oz) hazelnuts, skinned, toasted and chopped
double cream and extra toasted hazelnuts, to serve

Melt the butter, add the onions and potato and cook gently until softened. Add the chicken stock and bay leaves and simmer for about 10 minutes until the potatoes are very soft.

Stir in the sprouts and hazelnuts and simmer for 6-8 minutes until the sprouts are tender but still green. Liquidise, season to taste with salt and pepper. If the soup is a little thick, add some more stock.

Reheat and serve with a swirl of cream and extra hazelnuts.

SERVES 6.

LEFT: Top, barszcz z uskami, a clear beetroot soup from Poland and bottom, Brussels sprout and hazelnut soup. Barszcz is traditionally made by fermenting beetroot with rye bread for a week but this simple recipe is just as delicious.

VARM RÖKT LAX MED SMÖR

FOR THE SAVOURY BUTTER:
75 g (3 oz) softened butter
grated rind and juice of ¹/₂ lemon
30 ml (2 tbsp) chopped fresh dill or
5 ml (1 tsp) dried
30 ml (2 tbsp) capers, drained and
finely chopped
900 g (2 lb) smoked salmon
lemon wedges and sprigs of dill, to
garnish

Cream the butter and beat in the remaining ingredients. Form a roll and wrap in damp greaseproof paper or kitchen foil. Chill.

Lay the smoked salmon on a sheet of kitchen foil and season with black pepper. Cover with another sheet of foil and seal the edges. Place on a baking sheet and heat in the oven at 220°C (425°F) Gas mark 7 for 15-20 minutes. Arrange on a platter and serve with sliced savoury butter. Garnish with lemon wedges and dill.

SERVES 4-6.

DORADE AUX OLIVES

This dish is served on Christmas Eve in Southern France.

1.1 kg (2¹/₂ lb) red snapper (or grey
mullet, sea bass or red mullet)
1 medium fennel bulb, diced
¹/₂ lemon, sliced
2 bay leaves
olive oil
1 small onion, sliced
2 garlic cloves, skinned and finely
sliced
about 45 ml (3 tbsp) plain flour
175 g (6 oz) Greek-style black olives,
pitted
60 ml (4 tbsp) Pernod or white wine
salt and pepper
30 ml (2 tbsp) chopped fresh parsley,
lemon slices and fennel tops, to garnish

Scale and clean the fish and stuff with the fennel, lemon and bay leaves. Tie around the middle with fine string.

Heat 45 ml (3 tbsp) olive oil in a frying pan and add the onion and garlic. Cook until soft but not coloured. Spoon into an oval oven-proof dish that will take the fish.

Roll the fish in the flour and lightly brown in a little olive oil. Place on top of the onion. Add the olives and Pernod and season lightly. Cover with oiled kitchen foil and bake at 180°C (350°F) Gas mark 4 for about 20 minutes, basting frequently. Sprinkle with parsley. Serve garnished with lemon slices and chopped fennel tops.

SERVES 4-6.

RIGHT: Varm rökt lax med smör or hot smoked salmon with savoury butter. The Swedish Christmas Eve celebrations begin with the customary Christmas toast followed by a smörgåsbord — a large buffet of hot and cold foods that can be eaten with bread and butter. Lax (salmon), either marinated or smoked, is always a part of this feast.

MEXICO

ENSALADA DE NOCHE BUENA

1 medium iceberg lettuce
3 oranges
large red apple
2 bananas
175-225 g (6-8 oz) fresh cooked
beetroot, peeled
175-225 g (6-8 oz) fresh pineapple
chunks
175 g (6 oz) roasted peanuts
1 pomegranate, peeled and seeds
extracted
150 ml ($^1/_4$ pint) French dressing

Shred the lettuce finely and arrange on a flat serving dish. Peel the orange like an apple and cut out the segments, leaving behind any membrane. Core the apple and cut into large chunks. Peel and slice the bananas. Dice the beetroot.

Arrange the prepared fruit and beetroot attractively on top of the lettuce. Sprinkle with the peanuts and pomegranate seeds. Spoon over the French dressing and serve immediately.

SERVES 6.

RIGHT: Top, dorade aux olives (red snapper with olives); bottom left, varm rökt lax med smör (warmed smoked salmon with savoury butter); and bottom right, ensalada de noche buena (Mexican Christmas salad).

ITALY

ITALY

FALSOMAGRO

This Sicilian Christmas dish sometimes known as 'Farsumauru' or 'false lean' – lean meat with a rich filling. It is made with a single lean piece of meat, beaten out, spread with stuffing, rolled and roasted. The fillings can be very elaborate, but this is a simplified version.

900 g (2 lb) thick slice beef topside
225 g (8 oz) rindless streaky bacon

FOR THE STUFFING:
225 g (8 oz) minced beef
225 g (8 oz) minced pork
50 g (2 oz) fresh white breadcrumbs
5 cloves garlic, skinned and finely chopped
30 ml (2 tbsp) chopped fresh parsley
30 ml (2 tbsp) freshly grated Parmesan cheese
1 egg, beaten
salt and pepper
30 ml (2 tbsp) seasoned flour
25 g (1 oz) butter
30 ml (2 tbsp) olive oil
300 ml (1/2 pint) red wine

With a sharp knife, cut the meat open horizontally (this is called butterflying) and spread flat between sheets of cling film. Beat out with a rolling pin until about 1 cm (1/2 in) thick. Cover the surface with the bacon.

To make the stuffing, mix the beef, pork, breadcrumbs, garlic, parsley, cheese and and egg together. Season well and spread in an even layer over the bacon, keep-ing the edges free. Roll the meat up like a Swiss roll and tie neatly at intervals. Roll the meat in the seasoned flour.

Heat the butter and oil in a flameproof casserole, add the beef and brown well all over. Add the wine, cover tightly and cook at 180°C (350°F) Gas mark 4 for 1½ hours, adding more liquid from time to time.

Serve the beef sliced with the juices, accompanied by creamy mashed potatoes and sautéed mixed mushrooms.

SERVES 6-8.

ABOVE: Falsomagro is a garlicky stuffed beef dish served in Sicily as a main dish on Christmas Day, shown here served with colourful sautéed mushrooms.

CANADA

WINTER VEGETABLE GRATIN

butter
350 g (12 oz) mixed turnips, swede
and parsnips, peeled and sliced
2 dessert apples, peeled cored and
sliced
freshly grated nutmeg
salt and pepper
30 ml (2 tbsp) soft brown sugar
about 300 ml (¹/₂ pint) double cream
50 g (2 oz) fresh breadcrumbs

Butter a shallow ovenproof dish. Blanch the vegetables in boiling water for 3 minutes. Drain and cool slightly. Layer the apple and vegetables alternately in the dish, dotting with butter and seasoning with nutmeg, salt and pepper. Pour in enough cream to just cover the vegetables. Sprinkle with the sugar then the breadcrumbs and bake at 180°C (350°F) Gas mark 4 for 30 minutes until golden.

SERVES 4-6.

RIGHT: Top, winter vegetable gratin and below, a delicious serving dish of sliced falsomagro. Root vegetables may be humble on their own, but in this Canadian gratin dish they make a delicious accompaniment to a rich main course.

GERMANY

SCHWEINEROLL-BRATEN MIT PFLAUM

2 dessert apples, peeled, cored and sliced
8 large plums, pitted and chopped
pinch of cinnamon
2.5 ml ($^1/_2$ tsp) soft brown sugar
50 g (2 oz) fresh brown breadcrumbs
salt and pepper
1.4 kg (3 lb) boned pork loin, skin removed
25 g (1 oz) butter
30 ml (2 tbsp) olive oil
2 bay leaves
150 ml ($^1/_4$ pint) white wine
extra plums and bay leaves, to garnish

Mix the apples, plums, cinnamon, sugar and breadcrumbs together. Season to taste with salt and pepper. Lay the meat skin-side down and spread the stuffing over the flat part where the bones have been removed. Roll up and tie neatly.

Heat the butter and oil together in a flameproof casserole and brown the meat all over. Add the bay leaves and wine, cover tightly and simmer over a gentle heat for about 2 hours.

Slice the meat thickly and serve, with the skimmed juices. Garnish with plums and bay leaves.

SERVES 6-8.

DENMARK

RØDKÅL

900 g (2 lb) red cabbage
25 g (1 oz) butter
1 small onion, peeled and finely chopped
30 ml (2 tbsp) soft brown sugar
60 ml (4 tbsp) raspberry wine vinegar
salt and pepper
freshly ground nutmeg
30 ml (2 tbsp) redcurrant jelly
1 apple, peeled, cored and grated

Halve and remove the core from the cabbage. Shred finely and soak for 5 minutes in cold water. Drain well. Melt the butter in a flameproof casserole and cook the onion until golden. Stir in the cabbage, sugar and the vinegar. Season to taste with salt, pepper and nutmeg.

Cover tightly and simmer over a low heat for about 1$^1/_2$ hours, adding a little water from time to time to keep it moist. Add the redcurrant jelly and apple 15 minutes before the end of cooking.

SERVES 6.

USA

BUTTERNUT SQUASH WITH MAPLE SYRUP

Serve this as a starter, or a supper dish. Smaller squashes could be baked as accompaniments to roast turkey and other main courses.

2 small butternut squashes, halved and seeds removed
25 g (1 oz) soft brown sugar
1.25 ml ($^1/_4$ tsp) ground mixed spice
pinch of salt
25 g (1 oz) butter, melted
75 ml (5 tbsp) maple syrup
8 thin slices rindless streaky bacon

Place the squash cut side up in a baking dish. Mix the sugar, spice, salt, butter and maple syrup together and spoon into the squash. Twist the bacon and lay across the squash.

Pour a little water around the squash and bake at 180°C (350°F) Gas mark 4 for about 30 minutes or until tender. Baste the bacon and squash with the maple syrup twice during cooking.

SERVES 4.

LEFT: Schweinerollbraten mit Pflaumen (a roll of pork stuffed with plums) is a typical festive dish from Germany which would be served with braised red cabbage and rice with apricots and onions.

LEFT: Top, Schweinerollbraten mit Pflaumen garnished with plums and bay leaves; right, rødkål, a piquant red cabbage side dish which includes redcurrant jelly and apple; and bottom, butternut squash with maple syrup.

GREAT BRITAIN

ROAST TURKEY AND STUFFINGS

TRADITIONAL ROAST TURKEY

This is a real family-sized recipe, but if you are just one or two, try using smaller cuts of turkey such as breast fillets, steaks, turkey breast roast or leg roast.

5-8 lb fresh or frozen turkey, thawed
thoroughly
125-175 g (4-6 oz) butter, softened
salt and pepper

Prepare the stuffings in advance, but only stuff the turkey just before cooking.

Wash the bird thoroughly inside and out and dry with kitchen paper. Use one stuffing to stuff the neck flap and cook the other separately. (Place in a buttered ovenproof dish or roll into balls, fry and bake.)

Cover the surface of the turkey with softened butter to keep the breast moist. Line a large roasting tin with foil, bringing the edges over the rim. Place the turkey in the centre of the tin, covering it loosely with another sheet of foil, tucking the edges inside the rim. Roast at 180°C (350°F) Gas mark 4 for 3-3½ hours. Remove the foil for the last 30 mins to allow the skin to brown.

Test the deepest part of each thigh with a skewer to check that the juices run clear and the bird is cooked through. Allow to rest in a warm place for 15 minutes to make carving easier while making the gravy.

SERVES 6-10.

The traditional accompaniments to Roast Turkey are:
Brussels Sprouts with Chestnuts
Chipolatas wrapped with Bacon
Roast Potatoes
Bread Sauce
Cranberry Sauce
Turkey Gravy
Stuffing

STUFFINGS

All these stuffings can be used to stuff turkey or any seasonal bird such as goose or capon.

Oatmeal, Herb and Nut Stuffing

75 g (3 oz) butter
1 onion, peeled and chopped
175 g (6 oz) rolled oats
225 g (8 oz) toasted hazelnuts,
chopped
90 ml (6 tbsp) mixed chopped fresh
parsley, thyme and tarragon
175 g (6 oz) fresh brown breadcrumbs
finely grated rind of 1 lemon
1 egg, beaten
salt and pepper

Melt the butter and cook the onion until soft. Mix in the remaining ingredients. Season well.

Chestnut and Bacon Stuffing

75 g (3 oz) butter
1 onion, peeled and finely chopped
6 rashers rindless streaky bacon,
chopped
225 g (8 oz) cooked mixed grain rice
25 g (1 oz) pine nuts, toasted
450 g (1 lb) vacuum-packed chestnuts,
chopped
salt and pepper
pinch of ground mace

Melt the butter and cook the onion until soft. Mix in the remaining ingredients. Season well.

Prune, Pear and Walnut Stuffing

75 g (3 oz) butter
125 g (4 oz) chicken or turkey livers,
trimmed and chopped
450 g (1 lb) minced veal or pork
12 large no-soak prunes, pitted and
chopped
4 pears, peeled, cored and chopped
50 g (12 oz) walnuts, chopped
salt and pepper

Melt the butter and cook the livers for 1-2 minutes. Mix in the remaining ingredients. Season well.

LEFT: The traditional roast turkey provides a focal point for the traditional Christmas meal in many countries around the world. Here the seasonal bird, golden brown and succulent, is surrounded by several stuffing variations.

CHRISTMAS CAKES

*S*pecial cakes and sweetmeats are a universal and essential part of any celebration or festival and at Christmas every country serves its own specialities and treats. Old family recipes handed down through the generations are carefully followed and adapted to make seasonal delicacies using traditional ingredients. Dried fruits, nuts and spices dominate and are baked into yeasted breads and pastry confections. In Provence a ritual of serving thirteen desserts after the return from midnight mass is still followed and must be the ultimate sweet feast. The desserts are always left on the table until the Twelfth Night, replenished when necessary. The desserts include mandarins, fresh raisins and prunes, glacé chestnuts, small iced marzipan cakes and nougat made with honey and almonds.

SWEDEN

ST LUCIA'S SAFFRON BREAD

These pretty breads are eaten in Sweden on 13th December to mark the start of Christmas festivities. They are served with coffee when the candles are lit.

large pinch of saffron threads
15 ml (1 tbsp) active dried yeast
50 ml (2 oz) caster sugar
450 g (1 lb) plain white flour
large pinch of salt
50 g (2 oz) butter, melted
100 ml (4 fl oz) milk, warmed
2-3 drops vanilla essence
125 g (4 oz) raisins, chopped
2 eggs, beaten
extra raisins, to decorate
1 egg yolk, to glaze

Put the saffron in a small bowl, pour over 30 ml (2 tbsp) hot water and leave to infuse for 20 minutes. Sprinkle the yeast into 75 ml (3 fl oz) warm water and stir in 5 ml (1 tsp) of the sugar. Leave for 10 minutes until frothy.

Sift the flour and salt together into a bowl. Stir in the saffron water, melted butter, milk, sugar, vanilla, raisins and eggs. Mix to a soft dough. Turn out and knead for 5 minutes until smooth. Place in an oiled bowl, cover and leave to rise in a warm place for about 1 hour until doubled.

ST LUCIA'S SAFFRON BREAD (Sweden)

PANNETONE (Italy)

STRUCLA (Poland)

GALETTE DES ROIS (France)

SPECULAAS (Holland)

BUNUELOS (Mexico)

GLI SFRATTI (Italy)

ROSCON DE REYES (Spain)

STOLLEN (Germany)

BÛCHE DE NOËL (France)

MINCE PIES (Great Britain)

BLACK BUN (Scotland)

Knock down the dough, and knead until smooth. Divide into 8 pieces. Roll each into a long sausage and shape into 'S' shapes or back-to-back 'C' shapes as shown in the photograph. Decorate with raisins. Brush with egg yolk mixed with 5 ml (1 tsp) water and a pinch of salt. Place on baking sheets and leave to rise for 30 minutes until swollen.

Bake at 190°C (375°F) Gas mark 5 for 15-20 minutes until golden brown. Cool on a wire rack. Serve warm with coffee.

ITALY

PANNETONE

A Milanese Christmas bread which keeps well. It is cut in horizontal slices, the top being replaced and the whole wrapped so that it doesn't dry out, and refrigerated. A piece is kept aside to eat on 3rd February, the feast day of St Biagio, the protector of throats!

15 ml (1 tbsp) active dried yeast
150 ml (¼ pint) milk, warmed
about 450 g (1 lb) strong plain flour
10 ml (2 tsp) salt
75 g (3 oz) caster sugar
1 egg beaten with 4 egg yolks
175 g (6 oz) unsalted butter, softened
125 g (4 oz) raisins
finely grated rind of 1 lemon
finely grated rind of 1 orange
50 g (2 oz) chopped candied orange
and citron peel

Dissolve the yeast in 60 ml (4 tbsp) warmed milk. Leave for 10 minutes to froth. Stir in 125 g (4 oz) of the flour and the remaining warm milk. Cover and leave to rise for 30 minutes.

Sift the remaining flour and salt onto the yeast mixture. Make a well in the centre and add the sugar and beaten eggs. Mix to an elastic dough. Add a little more flour but keep the dough quite soft. Work in the softened butter. Cover and leave to rise until doubled in size. Knock down and leave to rise until doubled in size again. Work in the fruit. Line a 16 cm (6½ in) deep cake tin with a double strip of non-stick baking parchment which projects 12.5 cm (5 in) above the rim. Line the base with baking parchment. Place the dough in the tin, cut an 'X' on the top with a razor blade, cover and leave to rise until it rises 2.5 cm (1 in) above the top of the tin.

Bake at 200°C (400°F) Gas mark 6 for 15 minutes then lower the heat to 180°C (350°F) Gas mark 4 and bake for about 40 minutes until well-risen and golden. Leave the pannetone to cool in the tin for 10 minutes then transfer to a wire rack to cool.

Wrap and store in an airtight tin for up to 3 weeks.

LEFT AND FAR LEFT: Pannetone, an Italian Christmas bread, is surrounded by St Lucia's saffron bread formed into different swirling shaped buns which are delicately flavoured and coloured with saffron. Traditionally they are served by the eldest daughter to the rest of the family on St Lucia's Day, the 13th December. Pannetone can be served sliced or alternatively the middle can be scooped out and replaced with rich and delicious fillings.

61

POLAND

STRUCLA

FOR THE DOUGH:

15 ml (1 tbsp) active dry yeast
150 ml (¹/₄ pt) milk, warmed
50 g (2 oz) butter
75 g (3 oz) caster sugar
3 eggs
450 g (1 lb) plain white flour
2.5 ml (¹/₂ tsp) salt
15 ml (1 tbsp) rum (optional)
few drops of vanilla essence
finely grated rind of ¹/₂ orange

FOR THE FILLING:

150 g (5 oz) poppy seeds
50 g (2 oz) ground almonds
50 g (2 oz) raisins
75 g (3 oz) honey
60 ml (4 tbsp) caster sugar
1 egg yolk, to glaze
glacé icing, candied fruits and nuts to
decorate (optional)

Dissolve the yeast in the warm milk and leave for about 15 minutes until foamy. Cream the butter and sugar together then beat in the eggs. Make a well in the centre and pour in the yeast mixture, the butter and the flavourings. Mix together and knead until smooth. Cover and leave to rise until doubled in size. Knock down and leave to rise until doubled again.

To make the filling, put the poppy seeds in a pan and cover with boiling water. Leave to stand for 40 minutes. Strain through muslin or a fine sieve. Grind the seeds in a coffee mill or blender. Transfer to a bowl and stir in the almonds, raisins, honey and sugar.

Knock down the dough and roll out to a rectangle about 5 cm (½ in) thick. Spread the filling over the dough, keeping the edges free. Roll up from the short side and lift onto a baking sheet, seam side down. Mix the egg yolk with a little water and brush over the loaf. Bake at 190°C (375°F) Gas mark 5 for 20-30 minutes until golden. Leave in the tin for 10 minutes, then transfer to a wire rack to cool.

FRANCE

GALETTE DES ROIS

This Twelfth Night Cake has a bean or a 'santon' hidden inside it, and whoever finds it in their slice is king for the night. These cakes are sold in France decorated with a gold paper crown.

500 g (1.1 lb) good puff pastry
75 g (3 oz) butter, softened
100 g (3¹/₂ oz) caster sugar
200 g (7 oz) ground almonds
45 ml (3 tbsp) rum
2 small eggs, beaten
1 dried bean or lucky charm
beaten egg and salt, to glaze

Cut the pastry in two and roll each half to a thickness of 0.5cm (¼ in). Using a plate as a guide, cut out two 20 cm (8 in) circles. Roll one out a little larger than the other. Chill.

Cream together the butter, sugar, almonds and rum until pale and thick. Gradually beat in the eggs.

Place the smaller round of pastry on a wet baking sheet. Spoon the almond filling on top leaving a 2 cm (1 in) border. Push in the bean or charm. Moisten the edge with water and place the remaining round on top. Press the edges well to seal.

Decorate the top using the point of a sharp knife and brush with beaten egg. Bake at 220°C (425°F) Gas mark 7 for about 30 minutes, reduce heat to 190°C (375°F) Gas mark 5 for another 10 minutes. Serve warm or hot, decorated with a golden paper crown.

HOLLAND

SPECULAAS

These spiced sweetmeats are traditional Christmas fare in Holland, where they are eaten at the Feast of St Nicholas on December 6th.

FOR THE PASTRY:

250 g (9 oz) plain white flour
10 ml (2 tsp) mixed ground spice
pinch of ground cardamom
1.25 ml (¹/₄ tsp) baking powder
pinch of salt
150 g (5 oz) butter, cubed
125 g (4 oz) caster sugar
finely grated rind of ¹/₂ lemon
2 small eggs, beaten

FOR THE ALMOND PASTE:

225 g (8 oz) icing sugar
450 g (1 lb) ground almonds
1 egg, beaten
15 ml (1 tbsp) lemon juice

1 egg, beaten
50g (2 oz) blanched almonds, split

Sift the flour with the spices, baking powder and salt. Rub in the butter and stir in the sugar and lemon rind. Stir in the beaten eggs and bring together like pastry. Knead lightly. Wrap and chill.

Beat the almond paste ingredients together to form a stiff dough. Chill until firm.

Roll out the pastry to 3 mm (⅛th in) and cut two rectangles to fit an 18 x 28 x 4 cm (7 x 11 x 1½ in) deep baking tray. Place one in the bottom of the buttered tray.

Roll out the almond paste to fit the tin and place on top of the pastry. Cover with the remaining pastry layer. Brush with beaten egg and score the surface into diamond shapes with a skewer. Place a split almond on each diamond. Brush again with egg.

Bake at 180°C (350°F)/Gas mark 4 for 35 minutes or until golden. Cool slightly. Turn out of the tin, cool completely and cut into diamonds.

MAKES 30-40.

ABOVE: Top left, strucla, a poppyseed cake from Poland; top right, galette des rois from France; bottom, speculaas, spicy diamond-shaped cakes from Holland.

RIGHT: On Christmas Day, bunuelos, deep-fried sweetmeats, are sold in the main square in Mexico City.

FAR RIGHT: Top, roscon de reyes, a yeasted wreath-shaped cake decorated with colourful candied fruits; bottom left, gli sfratti, a honey-filled sweet from Italy; and bottom right, bunuelos.

MEXICO

BUNUELOS

In Mexico the bowls in which these doughnut-like fritters are served are smashed for good luck.

FOR THE SYRUP:
275 g (10 oz) dark soft brown sugar
300 ml (1/2 pint) water
1 stick cinnamon

FOR THE FRITTERS:
275 g (10 oz) plain white flour
2.5 ml (1/2 tsp) salt
2.5 ml (1/2 tsp) baking powder
15 ml (1 tbsp) caster sugar
1 egg, beaten
50 ml (2 fl oz) milk
30 ml (2 tbsp) butter, melted
45 ml (3 tbsp) Pernod

Place all the syrup ingredients together in a pan and simmer for 30 minutes. Set aside.

Sift the flour, salt and baking powder together. Stir in the sugar, egg, milk, melted butter and Pernod. Mix well and knead until smooth. Roll into walnut-sized balls, cover and leave to stand for 30 minutes.

Roll out into thin circles. Fry in at least 2.5 cm (1 in) of oil at 185°C (360°F) until puffed up and brown on both sides. Drain on kitchen paper, dip in hot syrup and serve in soup bowls. Serve extra syrup in a bowl.

MAKES ABOUT 60.

ITALY

GLI SFRATTI

This festive delicacy served in Tuscany dates from Etruscan times – the combination of honey and nuts is of very ancient origin.

FOR THE FILLING:
225 g (8 oz) honey
225 g (8 oz) walnuts or hazelnuts,
finely chopped
25 g (1 oz) fine breadcrumbs
finely grated rind of 1/2 lemon

FOR THE PASTRY:
50 g (2 oz) plain white flour
pinch of bicarbonate of soda
50 g (2 oz) granulated sugar
50 g (2 oz) butter, chilled and diced
1 egg, beaten
finely grated rind of 1/2 lemon
a little milk
egg yolk beaten with salt, to glaze

To make the filling, simmer the honey to reduce for 20 minutes. Stir in the nuts and cook for 10 minutes. Beat in the breadcrumbs and lemon rind. Chill.

Sift the flour and bicarbonate of soda together and stir in the sugar. Rub in the butter, mix in the egg and lemon rind to form a stiff dough. Add a little milk if the dough is too stiff. Knead lightly and chill for 30 minutes. Knead the dough and roll out thinly and cut into 4 strips, 30.5 x 7.5 cm (12 x 3 in) wide.

Divide the filling in 4. Roll each quarter to a sausage 30.5 cm (12 in) long and place one on each strip of dough. Roll up lengthways into 4 long sausages. Place seam-side down on a greased baking sheet and brush with beaten egg yolk.

Bake for 15-20 minutes at 200°C (400°F) Gas mark 6 until golden. Cool on a wire rack and cut into 2.5 cm (1 in) lengths.

MAKES 48.

SPAIN

ROSCON DE REYES

This is a yeast cake served on Twelfth Night. In Spain, presents are brought by the Three Kings, not Father Christmas. The cake has a little bean or charm hidden in it and is cut into equal slices and covered with a napkin to give equal shares. The guest who finds the bean is 'king' for the night and directs the festivities.

FOR THE STARTER:
15 g (1 tbsp) active dried yeast
5 ml (1 tsp) caster sugar
90 ml (6 tbsp) milk, warmed
50 g (2 oz) plain white flour

FOR THE DOUGH:
200 g (7 oz) plain white flour
2.5 ml (¹/₂ tsp) salt
50 (2 oz) caster sugar
finely grated rind of ¹/₂ orange
finely grated rind of ¹/₂ lemon
50 g (2 oz) butter, cubed
2 eggs (size 3) beaten
10 ml (2 tsp) orange flower water
10 ml (2 tsp) dark rum
dry bean, coin or lucky charm
beaten egg white, to glaze
flaked almonds and colourful candied
fruit to decorate

To make the starter, sprinkle the yeast and sugar onto the warm milk. Mix well and stir in the flour. Cover and leave to rise for 20 minutes until frothy.

For the dough, sift the flour and salt into a bowl, stir in the sugar and citrus rinds. Rub in the butter. Make a well in the middle and add the eggs, flower water, rum and starter.

Mix to a very sticky dough, then beat with your hand or in an electric mixer with a dough hook until smooth and elastic and the dough leaves the sides of the bowl. Cover and leave to rise for about 1 hour until doubled in size. Knock back, knead in the charm and shape into a long sausage. Place in a 23 cm (9 in) spring-form ring mould. Cover and leave to rise for about 1 hour until puffy.

Brush with egg white and scatter nuts and chopped candied fruit over the top. Bake at 180°C (350°F) Gas mark 4 for 30 minutes or until risen and golden brown. Cool in the tin for 5 minutes then turn out onto a wire rack to cool completely.

RIGHT: Top, slices of Stollen, a German Christmas loaf enriched with dried and glacé fruits and almonds. Bottom, bûche de Noël from France echoes the Christmas tradition of the Christmas log which was set alight at the beginning of the festivities and kept burning throughout.

FAR RIGHT: Chocolate leaves and meringue mushrooms are used to decorate the bûche in keeping with a woodland theme.

GERMANY

STOLLEN

This fruit- and nut-filled yeast bread is usually served at Christmas and holidays in Germany. When eaten at Christmas it is called 'Weihnachts-stollen'.

FOR THE DOUGH:

500 g (1 lb 2 oz) strong plain white flour
5 ml (1 tsp) salt
15 ml (1 tbsp) active dried yeast
200 ml (7 fl oz) milk, warmed
125 g (4 oz) caster sugar
175 g (6 oz) unsalted butter, melted
eggs, beaten

FOR THE FILLING:

75 g (3 oz) blanched almonds, toasted and chopped
50 g (2 oz) glacé cherries, quartered
50 g (2 oz) chopped mixed peel
75 g (3 oz) raisins
75 g (3 oz) sultanas
finely grated rind of 1 lemon
50 g (2 oz) ground almonds
25 g (1 oz) caster sugar
butter, melted
icing sugar, to decorate

Sift the flour and salt into a bowl. Sprinkle the yeast onto the milk and stir in 5ml (1 tsp) of the sugar. Leave for 10 minutes to become frothy.

Make a well in the centre of the flour and pour in the yeast mixture, sugar, butter and eggs. Mix well, cover and leave to rise for 30 minutes. Knock down, turn out and knead in the chopped almonds, cherries, peel, dried fruit and lemon rind.

Mix the ground almonds and sugar together. Divide the dough in two and roll each to an elongated oval, about 20.5 x 25.5 cm (8 x 10 in). Sprinkle the almonds over the dough and fold each almost in half lengthways, allowing the lower half to project by 5 cm (1 in). Brush with melted butter and leave to prove in a warm place until increased by half.

Bake at 190°C (375°F) Gas mark 5 for about 45 minutes. Cool slightly then brush with melted butter and dust with icing sugar. Cool completely on a wire rack and dust again with icing sugar.

FRANCE

BÛCHE DE NOËL

In France every patissière and boulangère has their own version of this Yule log; the variations are infinite. You can change the filling and cover the log with butter cream for a richer effect.

FOR THE ROULADE:

225 g (8 oz) plain chocolate
5 ml (1 tsp) instant coffee
5 large eggs, separated
150 g (5 oz) caster sugar
300 ml (¹/₂ pint) double cream
icing sugar, for dredging
extra icing sugar and caster sugar
chocolate leaves and meringue mushrooms, to decorate

Line a 23 x 33 cm (9 x 13 in) swiss roll tin with baking parchment. Melt the chocolate with the coffee and 60 ml (4 tbsp) water, stir until smooth.

Whisk the egg yolks and sugar until pale and light. Stir in the chocolate mixture. Quickly whisk the egg whites until stiff but not dry and fold into the chocolate mixture. Pour into the lined tin and spread evenly. Bake for 12-15 minutes at 220°C (425°F) Gas mark 7 until risen and firm. Cover with a damp cloth and leave to cool overnight in the tin.

Turn out the sponge onto a well-sugared sheet of greaseproof paper. Peel off the parchment, and trim off the edges. Cut a narrow strip off a shorter side for a knot. Whip the cream softly and spread over the roulade. Roll up from the shorter side. Don't worry if it cracks – this will give a good log effect.

Place the roulade on a plate. Use the trimmings and a little whipped cream to make a branch and attach with a little cream and a couple of cocktail sticks. Dust with extra icing sugar and caster sugar to look like snow.

Decorate with chocolate leaves and meringue mushrooms. Chill until ready to serve.

ABOVE: Mince pies are an essential part of the celebrations in Great Britain. The mincemeat filling can contain different mixtures of dried fruits, nuts and spices, often with a liberal amount of spirit added. Using pastry cutters in Christmas shapes to cut out the lids makes these pies look particularly special.

GREAT BRITAIN

MINCE PIES

450 g (1 lb) fresh or frozen shortcrust pastry
450 g (1 lb) mincemeat (see below)
1 egg white, beaten
caster sugar

Roll out the pastry thinly. Using a fluted cutter, stamp out about 16 rounds to line a bun tin. Press each round into the bun tin and fill with spoonfuls of mincemeat.

Brush the edges of the pastry with water and cover with the remaining pastry rounds. Seal the edges and cut a small air-hole in the centre of each pie. Brush with beaten egg white and sprinkle with caster sugar.

Bake at 200°C (400°F) Gas mark 6 for 15 minutes.

Repeat the glaze and return to the oven for 5 minutes. Cool on a wire rack. (See photograph for alternative decorations including a meringue and nut topping.)

MAKES ABOUT 12.

Apricot and Orange Mincemeat

275 g (10 oz) no-soak dried apricots, soaked overnight
grated rind and juice of 1 orange
900 g (2 lb) mixed dried fruit
60 ml (4 tbsp) orange marmalade
450 g (1 lb) demerera sugar
225 g (8 oz) shredded vegetable or beef suet
7.5 ml (1½ tsp) mixed spice
1.25 ml (¼ tsp) grated nutmeg
200 ml (7 fl oz) brandy

Drain the apricots and finely chop. Mix with the remaining ingredients, cover and leave overnight. Pack into sterilised jars and seal. Mature for up to 6 months.

Fruity Whisky Mincemeat

125 g (4oz) blanched almonds, chopped
125 g (4 oz) no-soak dried apricots, chopped
50 g (2 oz) dried figs, chopped
50 g (2 oz) stoned dried dates, chopped
350 g (12 oz) cooking apples, peeled, cored and chopped
250 g (9 oz) sultanas
175 g (6 oz) shredded vegetable or beef suet
grated rind and juice of 2 oranges
10 ml (2 tsp) mixed spice
125 g (4 oz) soft dark brown sugar
300 ml (½ pint) whisky

Mix all the ingredients together, cover and leave overnight. Pack into sterilised jars and seal. Mature for up to 6 months.

Christmas Mincemeat

125 g (4 oz) dried apricots, chopped
125 g (4 oz) dried figs, chopped
125 g (4 oz) mixed peel, chopped
225 g (8 oz) currants
225 g (8 oz) raisins
225 g (8 oz) sultanas
225 g (8 oz) shredded vegetable or beef suet
175 g (6 oz) chopped mixed nuts
450 g (1 lb) demerera sugar
finely grated rind and juice of 1 orange
finely grated rind and juice of 1 lemon
150 ml (1 pint) dark rum

Mix all the ingredients together thoroughly and leave overnight to macerate. Pack into sterilised jars and seal. Mature for up to 6 months.

SCOTLAND

BLACK BUN

Black Bun is an incredibly dense spicy fruit cake served on Hogmanay (31st December) and after midnight to the 'first footers' of the New Year. It can be made in a loaf shape or as a round cake, the top incised with appropriate patterns.

FOR THE PASTRY CASE:
450 g (1 lb) plain white flour
pinch of salt
2.5 ml (½ tsp) baking powder
200 g (7 oz) butter, cubed

FOR THE DOUGH:
350 g (12 oz) raisins
450 g (1 lb) currants
175 g (6 oz) plain white flour

LEFT: Top and bottom right, individual mince pies decorated with festive cut-out shaped tops are delicious served warm when friends and family visit. According to popular legend your first bite of mince pie each year grants a wish. Bottom right, slices of black bun, a very dark rich fruit cake from Scotland. The cake is encased in a pastry shell to keep the juices and flavour from escaping.

10 ml (2 tsp) ground allspice
5 ml (1 tsp) cinnamon
5 ml (1 tsp) mixed spice
2.5 ml (1/2 tsp) ground black pepper
2.5 ml (1/2 tsp) baking powder
2.5 ml (1/2 tsp) cream of tartar
2.5 ml (1/2 tsp) salt
75 g (3 oz) soft dark brown sugar
50 g (2 oz) unblanched almonds, chopped
50 g (2 oz) chopped mixed peel
150 ml (1/4 pint) milk
30 ml (2 tbsp) brandy
beaten egg, to glaze

Make the pastry as for shortcrust pastry. Wrap and chill. Roll out two-thirds and use to line a 900 g (2 lb) loaf tin. Chill. Keep the remaining pastry for the lid.

Wash the raisins and currants, cover with tepid water and soak for 15-20 minutes. Drain and dry well. Sift and mix all the dry ingredients together, then stir in the dried fruit, nuts and peel. Add the liquid ingredients to bind, and pack firmly into the pastry case.

Roll out the remaining pastry, dampen the rim and cover with the pastry, sealing the edges well.

With a small pastry cutter make indentations in the surface of the pastry, not quite cutting through. Pierce right through to the base with a skewer several times. Brush with beaten egg mixed with a pinch of salt.

Bake at 170°C (325°F) Gas mark 3 for 2 hours, then reduce to 150°C (300°F) Gas mark 2 for a further hour. Test with a thin skewer - it should come out clean. Cool completely and store in an airtight tin to mature for 2 weeks before serving.

SERVES ABOUT 20-30.

CHRISTMAS PARTIES

Christmas is the time for entertaining, when we can enjoy the company of friends and relations and share with them the warmth and goodwill of the season. If you are hosting the party, no matter how informal you intend the event to be, plan and prepare beforehand so you have plenty of time to join in the fun with everyone else.

When you are planning what to eat, remember that buffet food should be easy to eat with a fork and small snacks and canapés should be easy to pick up with fingers. Make sure you have provided enough plates, cutlery and glasses and that they are gleaming clean. If possible arrange the food and drink at several serving points to avoid awkward bottlenecks and long delays and remember to set out plates and cutlery together on the table, within easy reach.

Cut pies and cakes into portions before the party begins, so you can rest assured that there is enough to go round and also prevent mess and crumbs littering the table. Decide ahead of time where to stack the dirty dishes and allocate a space for them if possible.

As a rough guide, allow about eight snacks per person and provide a cheese board and lots of French bread and a selection of raw vegetable crudités and dips if you are uncertain how many people are likely to turn up. Allow three to four glasses of wine or punch per person and always provide a selection of non-alcoholic drinks for the drivers and the children. Garnish ready-mixed beverages with fruits and spices to make them decorative and appetising, especially the non-alcoholic ones.

Traditionally in Anglo-Saxon times, the host would provide a Wassail bowl filled with an aromatic punch of hot ale with roasted apples floating on the surface. The apples, cooked in the liquid until they turned soft and fluffy, gave the drink its name of Lambswool. Beaten eggs, sugar spices and sometimes nuts were added to the brew with small pieces of toasted bread dropped in. When the party guests arrived, it was customary for the host to hold up the bowl and cry out 'Wes Hal' which meant 'Be Whole' or 'Be in Good Health'. The bowl would be passed around the guests who would reply 'I drink to your health'. The pieces of toast included in the drink gave the custom of 'raising a toast' its name. And so the custom continues as we lift our glasses to raise a toast and wish for fresh starts and new hope for the year ahead surrounded by friends and family.

PARTY INVITATIONS

ABOVE: Gold sealing wax adds the finishing touch to give a party invitation a stylish stamp.

*H*ome-made party invitations look extremely impressive and require only a small amount of time to make. Hand write the party details with a fountain pen and coloured ink for a really classic touch or use a gold or silver felt tip pen to follow the seasonal colour theme. Fold parchment around them and tie with narrow tape or ribbon like a flat parcel if they are to be delivered by hand, or for the finishing touch send them in tissue-paper-lined envelopes sealed with sealing wax.

CLASSIC GARLANDS

Reproductions of black and white engravings and drawings can be used to decorate stationery and are worth looking out for in books and magazines, especially drawings of garlands, borders and ribbons taken from the 18th and 19th centuries. Using a photocopier, the designs can be reduced or enlarged to fit within a postcard size. For the invitation with the fruit garland, carefully cut out the photocopied image with scissors, then cut an oval of plain white paper to fit within it, to make an area big enough for the party details to be written. Stick them onto coloured metallic card.

LACE STARS

Spray small paper doilies with gold and copper paint and leave to dry. Cut star shapes out of good-quality cartridge paper to fit within each doily and big enough to write the invitation details on. Thread a length of cord or fine braid through the top of the star and doily to join them together and tie a bow.

CUTLERY INVITATIONS

Knives, forks and spoons in glimmering colours make novel invitations. Spray plastic picnic cutlery in gold, copper and silver and attach labels, made from metallic card, to the handes with lengths of ribbon and fine braid, tied into bows.

BRAID AND CHRISTMAS STAR

Cut two lengths of flat gold upholstery braid to fit along the top and bottom of a rectangle of card and

thread each end through slits made in the card with a craft knife. Trim the ends short and secure at the back with glue, pulling the braid taut across the front. Sew a star bead to the centre of the top strip of braid to complete.

GOLD TASSELLED LABEL

Make a label out of gold card and attach a gold tassel to one end of it. Write the invitation details with a permanent ink felt tip pen.

SLOTTED RIBBON BORDER

Decorate a plain card by adding a slotted ribbon border. Cut slits in pairs all around the edge of the card and thread the ribbon through them, beginning and ending at a corner. Tie the ribbon into a bow and trim the ends.

RIGHT: Photocopied motifs taken from old black and white engravings can be used to create classic party invitations with a period feel.

FAR LEFT: The braid and Christmas star invitation uses grosgrain braid to make a simple border along the top and bottom edges of a card with a gold star bead sewn at the centre top to complete.

LEFT: An impressive array of party invitations. Clockwise from top left, classic garlands copied from old engavings make stylish cards; the braid and Christmas star design has an imperial feel; a lace star made from a spray painted doily; cutlery invitations made from picnic knives, forks and spoons; a gold tasselled label and a pretty invitation with a slotted ribbon border.

TABLE DECORATIONS

For the Christmas dinner table a sumptuous arrangement of fresh flowers that catch the candlelight looks stunning. Choose a brass or copper container and gold candles, with richly coloured blooms that combine hues of deep reds and pinks, and finish it off with a rosette made from metallic ribbon, for a centrepiece that is flamboyant and glimmering. Never leave burning candles unattended and make sure to extinguish the candles before the flames burn down to the level of the foliage. The same technique can be used to make arrangements at other times of the year as well.

You will need: approximately 10 parrot tulips and 6 ranunculas for the flowers, berried ivy and box for the foliage, a shallow oval leak-proof container, chicken wire, sphagnum moss, 4 candles, reel wire, thin garden stakes (used to support plants), florist's scissors, wire cutters, a length of wide metallic ribbon, a piece of stub wire.

Cut an oblong of chicken wire, approximately twice the size of the container, and lay it flat. Place a quantity of sphagnum moss in the centre of the chicken wire and pull the edges together to completely enclose the moss and form an oval shape the same size as the container. Push the wire-enclosed moss into the container, bending it to fit, then put a small amount of moss on the top to completely conceal the wire.

Cut the garden stakes into 8 lengths, so each stick is 1½ times the depth of the container. Attach 2 sticks to the base of each candle by placing a stick on each side, running down the bottom 5 cm (2 in) of the candle to make 2 prongs sticking out from the base. Bind tightly around them with reel wire to hold everything together. Position the candles and push them into the moss so that they are held firm by the chicken wire.

Cut the foliage into lengths approximately twice the depth of the container and push them into the moss, around the candles, to make the outline shape for the arrangement. Cut the flower stems slightly shorter than the foliage and arrange them evenly within the shape, pushing them into the moss.

RIGHT: The materials you will need to make a striking focal point for the Christmas table. A piece of chicken wire crumpled and pushed inside an oval, leak-proof container provides a firm base to hold the stems in place.

To make the rosette, make a loop at one end of the ribbon 10 cm (4 in) deep and wind reel wire twice around the two thicknesses of fabric, at the open end, to hold and gather it together. Make another loop, the same size, to the side of the first one and wind the wire around it. Continue in this way until there are five loops held together at the centre with wire, to form a rosette.

Bring the end of the ribbon over the middle to cover the wire and twist the wire around it at the back, then cut off any excess ribbon.

Push a length of stub wire through the back of the rosette, bend it double and twist it around itself close to the rosette. Trim the stub wire if necessary and push it into the arrangement, to fix the rosette in place. Finally, fill the container with water.

75

STENCILLED TABLECLOTH

Stencilling is an easy way to decorate a Christmas table-cloth for the celebration meal. Our design is made up of three individual motifs which can be used in lots of different combinations. A seasonal evergreen branch with berries makes a design for the corners, a scroll design can be stencilled in pairs to form lines, make right angles at the corners or outline a central panel, and a rosette can be used between the scrolls or in the corners of the napkins, or alternatively, dotted evenly all over the cloth to fill large areas with pattern. Finding fabric that is wide enough to make a tablecloth can be a problem. For a large table use a sheet or a plain ready-made tablecloth, then stencil your design onto it. Or make a smaller overcloth, out of wide dress fabric, to go across the middle of the table over a larger, plain or damask cloth, like the tablecloth shown in the picture. It is made from bright pink organdie shot with gold, which shimmers with the gold stencilling to give an overall effect that is delicate and transparent. The napkins are made from a silk fabric with a slight sheen, in dark red to complement the elegance of the cloth.

ABOVE: The stencils, a branch and berry design, a scroll and a rosette, can be used together in various combinations. Draw the outlines onto stencil card using a permanent felt tip pen then cut away the shapes with a craft knife.

RIGHT: For the napkin, a rosette was stencilled at each corner and in the centre with scrolls making borders along the sides.

You will need: 1.3 m of 112 cm wide fabric and a 54 cm (21 in) square of fabric for each of the napkins, stencil card, repositioning spray mount, gold spray paint, masking tape, newspaper, a permanent felt tip pen, a craft knife, sewing thread.

Copy the outlines from the templates shown on pages 94 and 95 and draw each design onto a separate piece of stencil card with a felt tip pen, then cut out the stencils with a craft knife. Stick strips of newspaper around the edges of the stencils, with masking tape, to prevent the spray paint going onto the fabric, then spray the wrong sides of the stencils with repositioning mount to make them tacky so they will hold tight to the fabric. Practise working the stencils on waste scraps of fabric before embarking on the real thing, pressing the stencil in place, then applying the spray paint in short bursts to gradually build up the density of the colour, keeping the paint light and slightly uneven. Carefully peel the stencil off the fabric.

Cut the fabric straight at the edges, following the grain. Fold the fabric to find the centre point, making light creases to provide guide lines for positioning the central motif, then stencil a rosette at this point. Stencil 4 scroll motifs at quarter points around the rosette, at right angles to each other and parallel with the edges of the cloth.

Stencil the branch and berry design in each corner of the cloth, pointing away from the centre and with the last leaf of each branch 12 cm (4¾ in) away from the edges of the fabric. Stencil a rosette in the middle of each side, each rosette's centre 17 cm (6½ in) in from the edge of the fabric, then stencil a scroll on either side of the rosette, running parallel to the side edges. Turn under a hem all around the cloth and stitch in place.

For the napkins, stencil a rosette in the centre and one at each corner, each rosette's centre 9cm (3¾ in) in from the sides, then stencil 2 scrolls pointing away from the corners and parallel to the sides. Turn under a hem on all sides and stitch in place.

RIGHT: A stencilled cloth in a rich mixture of metallic colours is a welcome departure from the usual combination of traditional red and green and brings a luxurious and opulent look to the Christmas table.

NAPKIN FOLDING

Folded napkins are fun for a dinner party. To give each place setting an individual treatment, choose a differently shaped fold for each of the guests or simply alternate two different folds around the table. The folds are easy to achieve, but it is worth practising ahead of time to get the knack.

Cotton damask or crisp linen fabrics hold the folds well. For impressive results use napkins that are no smaller than 50 cm (20 in) square, freshly laundered, ironed flat and starched, avoiding bold patterns which will mask the simplicity of the folds.

RIGHT: From left to right, the waves make a neat flat fold, the candle can be decorated with a ribbon bow, the circus easily fills the plate at each place setting and fleur de lys gives an impressive finish but is easy to achieve. Folded napkins in crisp cotton or linen fabrics add a distinguished note to the festive table setting and can be used for dinner parties at other times of the year as well.

THE CANDLE

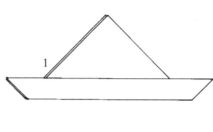

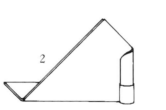

Fold the napkin in half diagonally to make a triangle with a wide base. Fold up 5 cm (2 in) all along the folded base edge (1) then turn the napkin over. Beginning at one base corner, roll the napkin tightly to form the candle (2), tucking the other base corner into the folds to hold the roll in place. Finish off the fold with a bow, if required.

THE WAVES

Fold the napkin into 3 to make a long rectangle and visualize 3 points dividing its length into half and quarters (1). Fold the short ends in to meet the quarter points (2), then fold in again so the folds meet in the middle (3). Turn the napkin over and fold in half again so 3 'waves' form along one edge. Pull the napkin back to spread the waves slightly apart.

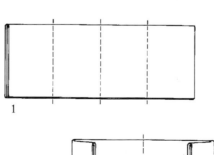

THE CIRCUS

Fold in the 4 corners of the napkin to meet at the centre and make a smaller square (1), then fold this in half to make a rectangle with all the napkin's edges inside it. With the open long side nearest you, hold the centre point of the top long folded side with your index finger and pull the top layer of the bottom left corner over to meet the bottom right corner, so it makes a triangle (2). Hold down the left half of this triangle and fold the other half back to bring the lower corners together again. Holding the centre top point as before, repeat the procedure on the other side by pulling the bottom right corner over to meet the bottom left corner and folding it back again to make a triangle (3). Pull the middle of the top folded layer at the triangle's base up to meet the top point, so the 2 bottom corners stand up then fold them down to meet in the middle (4). Turn the napkin over and repeat on the other side. Slide your left palm in between the folds on the left and fold the top layer up and over to meet its corresponding other half on the right. Turn the napkin over and repeat (5). Fold the top layer of the base edge up to meet the top of the shape, turn the napkin over and repeat on the other side (6). Hold up and with a finger in each of the 4 folds surrounding the centre point turn out the sides to make a cross and pull out the flaps.

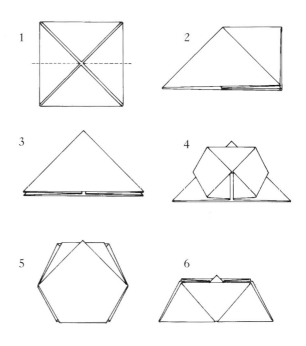

FLEUR DE LYS

This works best with a large napkin. Fold the napkin in half diagonally to make a triangle. With your index finger holding down the centre point of the triangle's base, fold the 2 bottom corners up to meet the top point (1). Fold the bottom point up by a third of the length to meet the folds down the centre (2), then fold the point back down to meet the base (3). Roll the sides around to the back pushing one side into the folds of the cuff on the other side to hold the shape in place and help it to stand up. Pull the top points down and tuck them into the sides of the cuff, then fold the front of the top point down to complete.

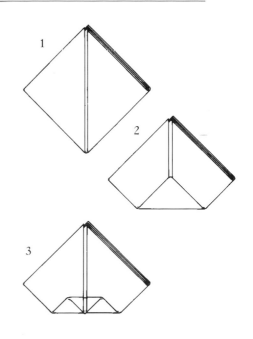

PARTY FOOD

PRAWN & GINGER FILO BASKETS

1 packet filo pastry
50 g (2 oz) butter, melted
350 g (12 oz) peeled prawns, finely chopped
5 ml (1 tsp) grated fresh ginger
4 spring onions, finely chopped
60 ml (4 tbsp) French dressing made with sesame oil
10 ml (2 tsp) toasted sesame seeds
salt and pepper
rings of spring onion, to garnish

Use a mini muffin tin and line each cup with three to four 6.5 cm (2½ in) squares of filo pastry, brushed with melted butter to form little frilly baskets. Bake at 190°C (375°F) Gas mark 5 until golden (about 15 minutes). Cool.

Mix together the prawns, ginger, spring onions, French dressing, sesame seeds, salt and pepper. Fill each case with a teaspoon of prawn mixture and garnish with spring onion rings. Crabmeat may be substituted for the prawns

MAKES ABOUT 30

TREASURE CHESTS

1 close-textured white loaf
butter, melted
45 ml (3 tbsp) soured cream
50 g (2 oz) jar black lumpfish roe
50 g (2 oz) jar keta caviar (salmon roe)
chives, to garnish

With a sharp, serrated knife, cut 8 rectangles measuring 5 x 3cm (2 x 1¼ in). Carefully cut an inner rectangle, cutting almost to the base of each rectangle, but not quite. Make a horizontal cut parallel to the base to free the inner rectangle. Carefully pull out the inner rectangle to form a box.

Brush liberally with butter and bake for 5-10 minutes at 180°C (350°F) Gas mark 5 until golden. Cool. Fill each box with a little soured cream and top with half black lumpfish roe, half keta caviar. Garnish with a cut chive.

MAKES 8.

ASPARAGUS & TAPENADE CROUTES

1 thin French stick
olive oil
125 g (4 oz) black olive paste
15 ml (1 tbsp) capers, drained
2 anchovy fillets, drained
pepper
30 ml (2 tbsp) olive oil
1 small garlic clove, skinned and crushed
40 thin asparagus tips, blanched

Thinly slice the bread diagonally, brush with olive oil and bake at 180°C (350°F) Gas mark 5 until crisp and golden. Cool. Pound the remaining ingredients together, except the asparagus. Spread the toasts thinly with the tapenade paste and top with crossed asparagus tips.

MAKES ABOUT 20.

RIGHT: Top left, asparagus and tapenade croutes; top right, treasure chests filled with black lumpfish roe and salmon roe; and bottom, prawn and ginger filo baskets. Small tasty containers made from filo pastry and baked bread can be filled with delicious savoury treats, and they are easy to pick up with your fingers, which is essential when serving party food.

ROASTED PEPPER & AUBERGINE PIZZETTE

2 red peppers
1 medium aubergine
45 ml (3 tbsp) olive oil
1 garlic clove, skinned and chopped
salt and pepper
1 packet pizza base mix
30 ml (2 tbsp) chopped mixed herbs
fresh marjoram, to garnish

Grill the peppers until blackened. Slip off the skins under cold water and remove the seeds. Dice finely. Finely dice the aubergine.

Heat the oil and fry the garlic and aubergine until golden, stir in the red pepper and season to taste. Make up the pizza dough according to instructions, adding the chopped herbs. Roll out very thinly and stamp out 5.5cm (2¼ in) rounds. Place on a baking sheet and top with a little aubergine mixture. Bake for about 8 minutes at 200°C (400°F) Gas mark 6 until golden. Cool and top with more filling before serving warm. Garnish with marjoram leaves.

MAKES ABOUT 20.

SMOKED SALMON TURBANS

8 slices (1 packet) rye bread or
pumpernickel
butter, softened
60 ml (4 tbsp) chopped fresh dill or
parsley
225 g (8 oz) long smoked salmon slices
lemon juice
freshly ground black pepper
dill sprigs, to garnish

Using a plain cutter, stamp out 16 4.5 cm (1⅓ in) rounds from the bread. Butter sparingly and roll the edges in the chopped herb. Cut the salmon into 16 strips 15 x 2.5 cm (6 x 1 in). Twist each strip and coil like a snake, then arrange to make a turban on top of the bread. Sprinkle with lemon juice and black pepper and top each with a dill 'feather'.

MAKES 16.

RIGHT: With a little care and attention to presentation, party food will look as good as it tastes. Top, smoked salmon turbans; centre right, roasted pepper and aubergine pizzette; and bottom, oriental chicken dolmades.

ORIENTAL CHICKEN DOLMADES

60 ml (4 tbsp) olive oil
1 bunch spring onions, finely chopped
225 g (8 oz) chicken breast, finely minced
225 g (8 oz) cooked mixed grain rice
2.5 ml (1/2 tsp) ground cumin
pinch ground allspice
30 ml (2 tbsp) chopped fresh parsley
30 ml (2 tbsp) chopped fresh coriander
75 g (3 oz) almonds, chopped
50 g (2 oz) no-soak apricots
salt and pepper
30 vine leaves in brine, soaked (or fresh if available)
fresh mint leaves, to finish

Heat the oil and fry the onion until soft and beginning to colour. Stir in the chicken and cook over a high heat, stirring to break it up. Stir in the remaining ingredients except the vine leaves. Season .

Place a teaspoon of filling on each leaf, fold in the edges and roll up to enclose the filling. Pack closely together, seam-side down in a shallow pan. Pour in 600ml (1 pint) water and a little extra oil. Place a plate on top to weigh the parcels down and to prevent them unrolling. Simmer gently for 20 minutes until tender.

Allow to cool in the liquid. When cold, transfer to the refrigerator to chill. To serve, wrap each one with a fresh mint leaf, spear with a cocktail stick, and arrange on a large platter.

MAKES ABOUT 30.

CHRISTMAS DRINKS

WINTER BLOSSOM

1 bottle sweet sherry
600 ml (1 pint) medium cider
50 g (2 oz) granulated sugar
5 cm (¹/₂ inch) fresh ginger, sliced
1 cinnamon stick
large pinch of freshly grated nutmeg
1 orange, thinly sliced
60 ml (4 tbsp) brandy
orange segments and cloves, to garnish

Heat everything together, except the brandy, in a large non-metallic pan until the sugar is dissolved. Just before serving, add the brandy and pour into heatproof glasses. Garnish with orange segments stuck with cloves.

SERVES 8.

VIN A L'ORANGE

3 large oranges, thickly sliced
1 small lemon, thickly sliced
1 vanilla pod, split
pinch of grated nutmeg
900 ml (1¹/₂ pints) light red wine
(11.5 -12% proof)
150 g (5 oz) granulated sugar
150 ml (¹/₄ pint) eau de vie or Polish
Pure Spirits (100-120% proof)

Put the first four ingredients into a large glass jar. Pour over the red wine. Seal and leave for about 6 weeks.

Strain through muslin and measure. Add 100 g (3¹/₂ oz) sugar per litre (1¹/₂ pints). Stir until dissolved then add the strong alcohol. Pour into 3 x 750 ml (1¹/₄ pint) sterilised bottles and cork. Store in a cool dark place for at least 1 month and up to 4 years.

GLØGG

1 litre (1 3/4 pints) red wine
450 ml (3/4 pint) Moscatel de Valencia
50 g (2 oz) fresh ginger, sliced
2 cinnamon sticks
6 cardamom pods, crushed
6 cloves
pared rind of 1 orange
100 ml (4 fl oz) vodka or aquavit
100 g (4 oz) sugar
100 g (4 oz) whole blanched almonds
175 g (6 oz) raisins

Put the first seven ingredients in a non-metallic saucepan and leave to infuse overnight. Heat slowly, adding the aquavit and sugar. Do not boil. Stir in the almonds and raisins and ladle into tumblers or mugs.

SERVES 8-10.

EGGNOG

6 large eggs, separated
175 g (6 oz) icing sugar
450 ml (3/4 pint) Jersey or full-cream milk
150 ml (¹/₄ pint) cognac
150 ml (¹/₄ pint) dark rum
thinly pared rind of 1 orange
grated rind of 1 lemon
450 ml (3/4 pint) double cream
freshly grated nutmeg

Whisk the egg yolks and sugar together until thick and pale. Stir in the milk, cognac and rum. Whisk the egg whites to soft peaks and gently fold into the mixture. Cover and chill for 2-3 hours.

Cut the orange rind into fine matchsticks. Whip the cream until barely thick. Stir this into the egg mixture and whisk until a little thickened. Stir in the grated lemon and half the orange. Pour into a punch bowl and scatter the remaining orange shreds over the top. Dust with grated nutmeg.

SERVES 12-15

LEFT: A fine selection of Christmas drinks, potent and aromatic. Eggnog is a rich concoction that includes cream, eggs, cognac and rum. Serve scattered with fine orange strands and dusted with nutmeg. Vin a l'orange has a long storage life so can be made well ahead of time. Winter blossom and glögg are heady and warming, perfect for a cold winter day.

PARTY HATS

RIGHT: Colourful paper hats can be decorated with beads, tassels and rosettes for stunning results. A four-pointed hat made from crepe paper is finished with a gold star at the end of each point.

The wearing of party hats can be traced back to the Roman Saturnalia when, as part of the celebrations, masters and slaves briefly changed roles. Saturnalia was a feast which was presided over by a Master of the Revels, sometimes called the Lord of Misrule and everything was turned upside down; the masters waited on their servants, men wore animal skins or dressed as women, and women dressed as men. The tradition was handed down and survived the centuries, ending up as part of the Twelfth Night festivities, when a man and woman were chosen at random to play the roles of king and queen and were given mock crowns to wear. Paper hats found inside Christmas crackers are now an accepted part of the fun but home-made hats are extra special.

You will need: crepe paper, coloured foil, medium-weight and thin card, scissors, glue, raffia, beads, feathers, ribbon.

THE CROWN

Cut a head band 3.5 cm (1½ in) deep out of medium-weight card, to fit around the head, adding an extra 3.5 cm (1½ in) overlap. Cut 2 strips of card 2.5 cm (1 in) deep and 40 cm (15½ in) long to make the crossed bands for the top of the crown. Cover one side of all these bands with gold foil, glued in place and

folded over to the wrong side. Glue the head band to form a ring, overlapping the ends, holding them in place with clothes pegs until the glue dries. Glue the crossed bands together at right angles to each other at the centre, then attach them to the ring, gluing the ends 3 cm (1¼ in) inside the band. Cut a 38 cm (15 in) circle out of crepe paper and gather all round the edge of it so it fits inside the head band and glue it in place inside the crown. Decorate with coloured foil diamonds and a pleated fan on the top.

POINTS AND STARS

Cut a head band 5 cm (2 in) deep out of thin card to fit around the head, adding an extra 3.5 cm (1½ in) overlap. Cut 4 pointed triangular shapes out of double sided crepe paper, with a base measurement that is one-quarter of the band

measurement plus 2.5 cm (1 in) added to each one, 26 cm (10¼ in) long and with the sides curving gently outwards towards the point. Glue the triangles to the wrong side of the band, overlapping and gluing them to each other to fit and placed 3.5 cm (1½ in) inside the band. Glue the band to form a ring, overlapping the ends. Cut another band out of coloured foil and glue it in place on the right side. Sew a star bead or stars cut out of card to each of the points.

POINTED HAT WITH ROSETTE AND TASSEL

Cut a head band as for the points and stars hat, out of foil. Cut 2 tall triangles out of crepe paper, each one in a different colour, 42 cm (16½ in) long with a base measurement that is half of the band plus 1 cm (⅜ in) for joining. Glue the triangles together down each side to form the hat and leave to dry. Glue the band around the bottom edge, then fold the hat in half lengthways and fold the top point down to meet the band. Decorate the point with a rosette and tassel.

TAM O' SHANTER

Cut a band 6 cm (2½ in) deep out of thin card, to fit around the head, adding an overlap of 3.5 cm (1½ in) and cut small flaps all along one long edge by making snips of 2 cm (¾ in), 1 cm (½ in) apart. Join the head band together, overlapping the ends and glue in place. Cut 2 circles out of crepe paper 32 cm (12½ in) in diameter. Take one of these circles and cut out a circle from the middle of it with a diameter the same as the head band and decorate the ring that remains with foil triangles. Glue the band to the ring by bending and gluing the flaps in place on the wrong side. Glue the remaining circle to the top

of it, joining it all around the edge. Cut a band of foil and glue it over the card band, then decorate at the front with a bow and feathers.

DIAMONDS AND TASSELS

Cut a band 5 cm (2 in) deep out of foil, to fit around the head, adding an extra 3.5 cm (1½ in) overlap. Cut a rectangle of crepe paper for the top of the hat, 3.2 cm (12½ in) long and with a width that is half

the band measurement plus 1 cm (½ in) for side turnings. Decorate one side of the rectangle with contrasting crepe paper diamonds and triangles, then fold in the side turnings, fold in half and glue the sides together. Decorate the band with contrasting crepe paper diamonds, then glue it around the hat, overlapping the ends. To complete, attach a tassel made from raffia to both top corners.

BELOW: From left to right, diamond and tassels; a regal crown; pointed hat with rosette and tassel; tam o'shanter with bright feather and ribbon decoration, and hat with points and stars.

PARTY GAMES

ABOVE: Marbles or alleys is a game that has been played by children since the middle ages and is still popular today. The marbles, alleys or taws, made of clay or glass, can be used to play different games all based on throwing or rolling them to hit the opponents' alleys out of the way or aimed to land within a target area or hole in the ground.

Traditional party games are lots of fun to play when friends and relations celebrate Christmas together. The Victorians dived for apples in tubs of water and played snapdragon, hunt the slipper, musical chairs and blind man's buff, as well as games involving cards and dice. Providing simple pleasure, games still hold their charm and enjoyment even in these times of television and computer games and there are a multitude of traditional games to choose from to incorporate into your family Christmas.

UP JENKINS

Traditionally this game is played with a sixpence, but any small coin will do. Any number of people can play. Two teams sit at opposite sides of a table. One team has the coin, which it must conceal from the other while obeying certain instructions given by the leader of the opposite team.

Team A starts with the coin, which is passed, beneath the table from hand to hand, until one player keeps it, hidden in his hand. On the order 'Up Jenkins' from the leader of team B, team A place their hands on the table, firmly clenched. The leader of team B can then call out any of the following three commands, which have to be carried out by team A:

Creepy Crawly – which means

move fingers forward in a crawling movement.

Wibbly Wobbly – clenched hands must be turned over and back on the table.

Flat on Table – hands must be laid down flat on the table.

Team B then guesses which member of team A has the coin. If they guess correctly it is their turn to conceal the coin. If they fail to guess, team A has another turn. The same player can keep the coin or pass it on to another player with their hands beneath the table again. The game continues in this way until the other team guesses who has the coin.

HEADS AND BODIES

Any number of players can take part and each will need a piece of paper, no smaller than 4 cm (1½ in) by 20 cm (8 in) and a pencil.

Each player draws a head on the top of their paper with a neck sticking down from it and folds the paper over so that only the neck is showing. The paper is then passed to the next person.

Each player then draws a body on the neck, finishing at the top of the legs and folds the paper over again, leaving the top of the legs showing. The papers are passed round again.

Next the legs are drawn, papers passed, and then the feet added. On the final time, each player

writes someone's name and folds the paper again. The papers are then jumbled up and each player chooses and unfolds one of them to see the results.

OLD MAID

Two or more players can take part. A pack of cards is required.

The Queen of Spades is taken out of the pack and put away, leaving 51 cards to be dealt out between the players. Each player looks at their cards and matches up any pairs that they have and puts them face down on the table.

The player on the left of the dealer then offers their cards to their neighbour to the left, holding the cards face down in a fan shape. The neighbour selects one and if it makes a pair with any of their hand, the cards are paired off and placed on the table as before.

This player then offers their cards to the next player, and so on, until all the cards are paired except one. The player left with the odd card is the old maid.

CONSEQUENCES

Any number of people can play. Each will need a slip of paper and a pencil and is asked to write down an adjective to describe a man. This done, the paper is folded to conceal the writing, and the papers are passed round to the next player on the left. Next comes a man's name, the papers are folded and passed. These are followed at each turn by another adjective, to describe a woman, a woman's name, the name of a place or building where they met, a remark made to the woman by the man, what her reply was, what the consequence was and finally what the world said.

The pieces of paper are then unfolded and read out as a story. If the members of the party are well acquainted with each other, the fun is greatly increased if their names and personal peculiarities are brought into play.

THE DREAM GAME

Any number of people can play. One person, who has never played the game before, is asked to leave the room on the understanding that the other players are going to think up a dream for them while they are outside. When they return they have to try and guess what dream has been chosen for them by asking questions. Unbeknown to them, no dream has been made up and their questions are answered using a simple technique; a question ending in a vowel is answered with 'yes', a question ending in a consonant is answered with 'no' and one ending with a 'y' is answered 'maybe'. The person unwittingly reveals their own deepest fantasies.

PELHAM

Any number of people can take part, only a pack of cards is required.

The cards are laid face down on the table, unsymmetrically, each card separate. The first player turns

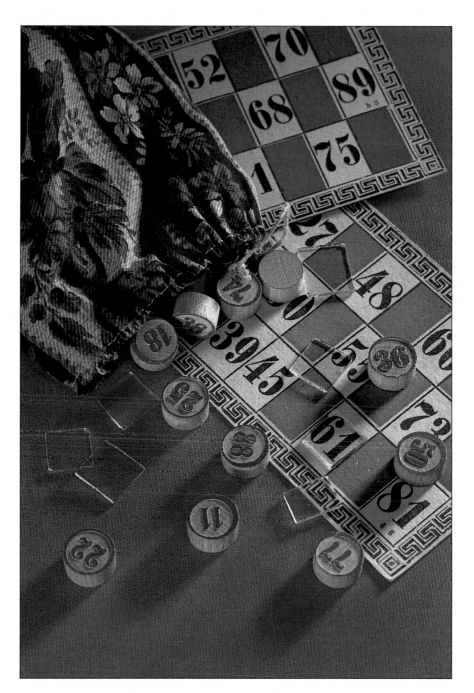

LEFT: For many families traditional party games are an essential part of the fun. Loto is a game for several players and is an older version of bingo. Each player has a card printed with squares and numbers and a dealer draws wooden counters from a bag and calls out the numbers. Glass counters are used to cover the numbers on the cards as they are called and the first person to cover all their numbers is the winner.

up one card, shows it to the others and replaces it, face downwards, as before then turns over another card and replaces it. Subsequent players likewise turn up 2 cards each, trying to remember which cards would make a matching pair to the first card turned. Pairs can be removed and kept by the player, who is then allowed another go. The winner is the player who ends up with the most number of pairs at the end.

CHRISTMAS COUNTDOWN

Planning ahead is the essence of a stress-free Christmas. Make your own timetable to follow before the celebrations get underway, to help avoid last-minute panics and enable you to relax and enjoy yourself. Many of the gifts and decorations can be made well ahead of time. Our countdown gives you a few guidelines on the ideal times to make your gifts, and your last chance to get started. Some of the gift preserves and vinegars need time to mature, but if you don't manage to make them in time to be ready by Christmas, don't despair; attach attractive labels giving information, including how long to store them for before opening, and they will still be much appreciated. Take the time to plan the meals you are likely to prepare over the holiday period, and cook as much of it as you can beforehand, freezing and storing wherever possible.

OCTOBER

Collect interesting-shaped jars and bottles to fill with *Rosemary and Lime Vinegar* and *Herb Vinegar*, *Layered Olives in Herb and Spice Oil* and *Whole Heads of Garlic in Olive Oil*.

Make *Christmas Vodka Liqueur*, *Prunes in Rum*, *Dried Figs in Brandy* and *Orange and Juniper Gin* and leave them to mature.

Make the *Mincemeats*.

Make *Pomanders*, turning them in their curing spices each day while they dry out.

NOVEMBER

Make *Pear Preserve* and *Cranberry Chutney*, using frozen cranberries if fresh are unavailable, and allowing at least 1 month to mature.

Make *Chocolate Truffles* and freeze them.

Vin a l'Orange keeps for up to 4 years, but needs a minimum of 1 month to mature, so make it now.

Many of the cakes can be baked and frozen up to 3 months beforehand. Make and freeze the *Bûche de Noël* without the filling and defrost and assemble the day before you need it.

Black Bun will keep in an airtight tin for up to 3 months, but you can make it now to give it time to mature.

Make *Mince Pies* and freeze them raw, freezing them in the tins before removing them to fill freezer bags. Cook on the day.

Make and freeze the soups, leaving the cream from the *Barszcz z Uszkami*; add it before serving.

Prepare the *Falsomagro* and *Schweinerollbraten* and freeze raw, cooking on the day.

Mix the turkey *Stuffings* and freeze them raw.

1st-5th DECEMBER

Make *Gift Boxes* and *Christmas Cards*.

Write and update your Christmas card list.

Plan your holiday menus.

Buy small gifts to fill homemade *Crackers* and *Advent Calendar*.

Freeze the biscuit bases for the *Treasure Chests* and *Asparagus and Tapenade Croûtes*, crisp them up in the oven and complete the making on the day.

Make up the *Roasted Pepper and Aubergine Pizzettes* and freeze them raw; bake them on the day required.

Bake and freeze the *Oriental Chicken Dolmades*.

6th-10th DECEMBER

Make *Tree Ornaments* and check that the electric tree lights are working. Buy replacement bulbs if necessary.

11th-15th DECEMBER

Choose and buy your Christmas tree and store it outside, or in a cold garage for a few days, standing it in a bucket of water.

Make *Lime Curd* and attach an 'eat by' label to each filled jar to let the recipient know how long it will keep.

Lebkuchen and *Swedish Spice Biscuits*

will keep in an airtight tin if you
make them now.

16th-20th DECEMBER

Bring the Christmas tree indoors
and decorate.

Wrap and label gifts to go under the
tree.

Gather or buy greenery to make
your *Wreath* and *Garland*. Keep
them in a cool place and spray
the leaves each day with water to
help keep them fresh.

Make the baskets for the *Prawn
and Ginger Filo Baskets* and keep
them in an airtight tin. Assemble
and complete them on the day.

20th-25th DECEMBER

Buy all the ingredients for your holiday menus.

Make last-minute gifts.

Buy flowers for your *Table
Centrepiece*, cutting 2.5 cm (1 in)
off the ends of the stems and
leaving them in deep water in a
cool place until ready to assemble
the display.

6th JANUARY

Take down the Christmas decorations, pack and store the ornaments and tree lights.

Discard the wreath and garland,
adding them to your compost
heap if you can.

TEMPLATES

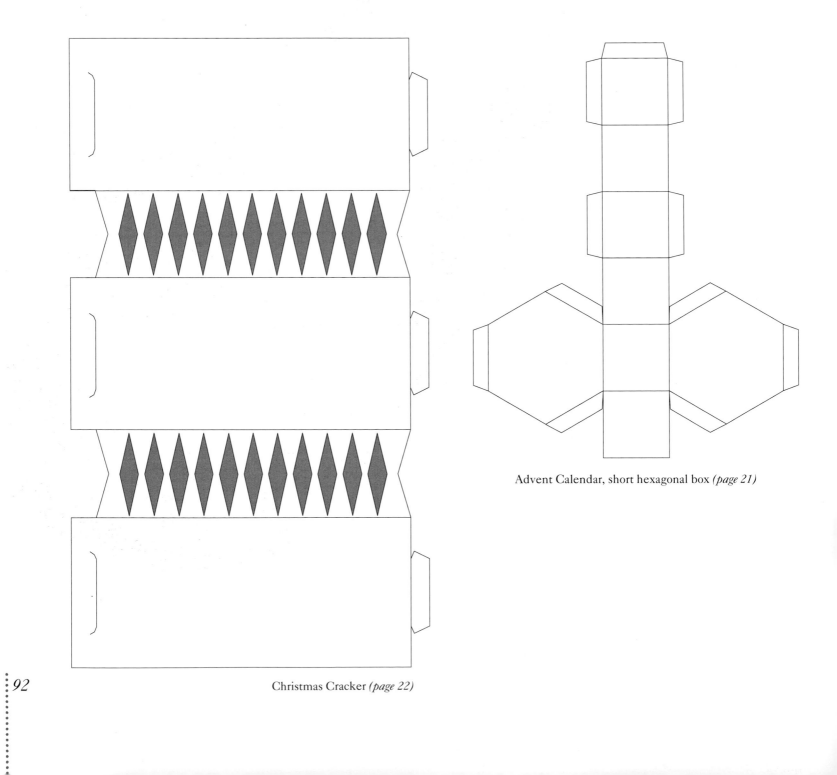

Christmas Cracker *(page 22)*

Advent Calendar, short hexagonal box *(page 21)*

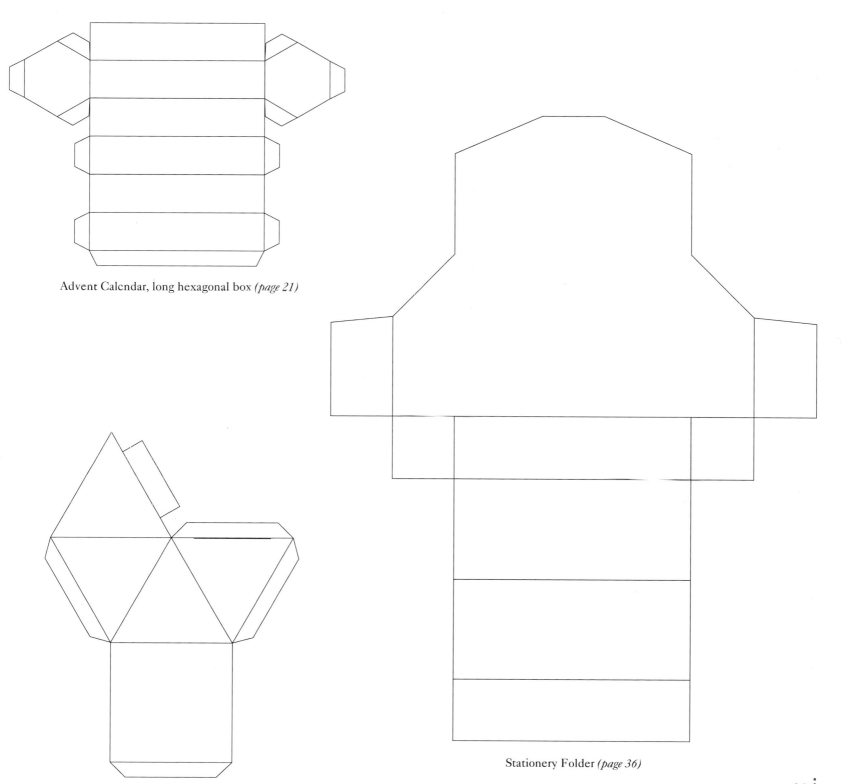

Advent Calendar, long hexagonal box *(page 21)*

Advent Calendar, Pyramid box *(page 21)*

Stationery Folder *(page 36)*

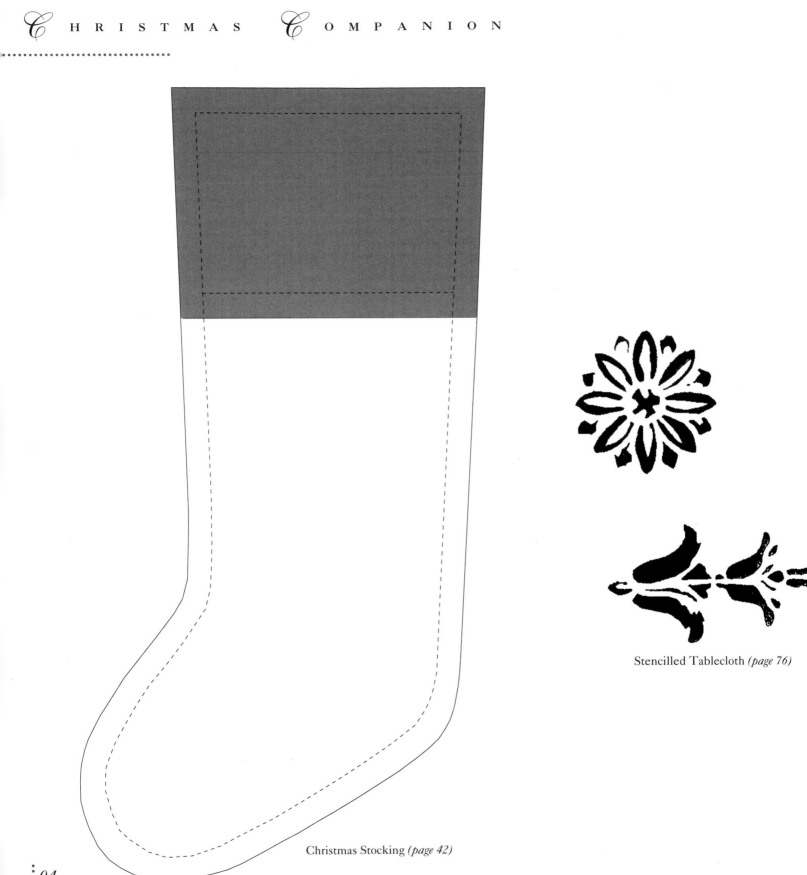

Stencilled Tablecloth *(page 76)*

Christmas Stocking *(page 42)*

Stencilled Tablecloth *(page 76)*

Rag Doll *(page 38)*

BODY

DRESS BODICE

SHOE

95

INDEX